Master the Art of TikTok
How to Go Viral and Build Your Brand

Copy Right

Table of Content

Introduction ………………………… **4**

Chapter

1. Understanding the basics of TikTok……………………….. 7

2. Lay the foundation of success…………………………. 20

3. Building Interesting Narrative………………………. 34

4. The Power of Hashtags and Captions….. ………………………………… 51

5. Monetizing your TikTok Presence……..………………….. 67

6. Case Studies of TikTok success…………………….… 81

7. Growing User Base and Engagement on TikTok…………………….90

8. Creating a Consistent Brand Image………….,,,,,………… 108

9. Global Reach and Diversity on TikTok..............…............128

10. Educational Resources and Algorithm Tips..….............145

11. Avoiding Common Pitfalls….............................…...159

12. Future Trends and Opportunities…........................…..178

Introduction

Within the largely ever-changing domain of social media, there exists one platform that has bewitched its collective conscience and redefined the very meaning of content creation, as well as content consumption: 'TikTok'. Its stratospheric rise in recent years has been such that TikTok today stands to be something much more significant than merely an app-it is an entire cultural movement, and its influence on billions of its worldwide users is almost without precedent. From viral dances to comedy skits, from tutorials to touching storytelling, TikTok's expanse of material textbookishly reflects the wildly imaginative and very resourceful global community of its users.

In the current digital age, where the attention of people is as short as the blink of an eye, with competition in capturing people's attention on the prowl, the art of TikTok mastery has ceased to be a luxury to become an imperatively strategic one for individuals and brands alike. Whether you are a first-time content creator and want to get your face out there in that digital space or a seasoned marketer and want to tap the potential of this ever-fast track platform for developing one's brand-centric engagements, this shall be the ultimate guidebook for you intended to help navigate this fast-changing world of TikTok.

Within these pages, you'll embark on a journey of discovery and empowerment, unlocking the secrets to viral success and brand-building prowess. We'll delve deep into the essence of TikTok – from its humble beginnings as a platform for lip-sync videos to its evolution into a powerhouse of creativity and influence. In return, you will understand TikTok's unique environment in a nuanced way, unravel the intricacies related to the algorithm, and explore its wide opportunities for content creators and brands.

But beyond a simple theoretical exploration of these mechanics at work on TikTok, this book also serves as a clear, actionable roadmap to drive tangible results in the digital space. Through its emphasis on expert insights, top-level strategies, and real-world use cases, you'll learn how to develop the sort of content that resonates with today's audience members, optimize your TikTok profile for maximum visibility, and harness the full capabilities of hashtags, trends, and analytics in a manner which lets you reach more people and make a dent in their lives.

Further, the book is a tribute to the magic of community and collaboration. In celebration of TikTok's magic, as you now begin a journey on the platform with me, you're coming aboard an energetic community of creators, marketers, and other like-minded enthusiasts sharing my passion for creativity, innovation, excitement, and fun. Together, we'll share success, overcome obstacles, and cross-pollinate one another in an ever-growing universe towards a hallmark of excellence in this boundless field of TikTok.

Take this book, then, as your trusty companion on that quite exhilarating adventure that is TikTok mastery-whether you're a digital native with something to say to the world or a mature brand not about to let your guard down. Let us embark on a journey of imagination, community, and endless possibility together within this remarkable platform and unlock its full potential. Welcome to the fine art of TikTok - where dreams become a reality and the world dances to your drum beat.

CHAPTER 1

Understanding The Basics Of TikTok

This chapter will take us into the world of a platform that has taken the internet zone by storm since its establishment. Just think about how a cat video and dance challenge dominated the digital landscape, all thanks to ByteDance and their masterstroke of genius. We are deconstructing this magically euphoric TikTok "For You" Charm. Every single tap and swipe brings before you a completely customized feed—all about you. Here's your time to gear in and plunder TikTok's treasure trove features. We will be your trusty guides through the TikTok interface jungle and make sure you emerge unscathed and fully equipped to conquer the digital realm like one who's made of the very stuff that stars are made of; A pro.

1.1 What is TikTok

TikTok is among the social media platforms that have revolutionized making and sharing digital content. It was developed in 2016 by Revolutionary Chinese Tech Giant ByteDance; it allows its users to create and share short videos, usually lip-sync to music 15 to 60 seconds long and other features. What sets TikTok out is that it is a presentation: a mix of entertainment, creativity, and community, wrapped up in an exceedingly user-friendly app. No less, it has absorbed the attention of millions of users globally. Especially the younger generation.

The magic of TikTok arises from such spontaneity and authenticity. Quickly, users record themselves dancing, lip-syncing, performing comedy skits, or showing some exceptional talent. The vast suite of editing tools, effects, and filters available means that, for anybody, regardless of technical abilities, video making has become democratically accessible. This ease has balanced the ability to have a myriad of voices and talents showcased.

A central feature of TikTok is the "For You" page, a custom feed that filters content according to an individual user's tastes and interactions. The advanced algorithm that is employed guarantees satisfaction with just what exactly is being sought, such that no two users are fed the same content in their interests, making the app highly addictive. Unlike many other social media applications and sites, TikTok doesn't have a discovery feed based on the count of followers and, instead, uses content quality and user participation to develop its algorithm. This means that any video could create a viral sensation, giving everybody a chance, especially the new breed of creators, to shine and become seen.

The rapid growth of TikTok may also primarily result from the energetic and participatory culture of its application. Due to this, mainly revolving around trends and challenges, the users will be able to develop and replicate altogether the patterns of a given dance, some theme, or even activity. This feeling of belonging and, at the same time, kindling the very viral nature of the content among a community spreads wider when brands, influencers, and even "common" users focus more attention on fueling these wildcats for more visibility. The loop continues.

TikTok is not like any other social media app; it is a cultural phenomenon that has brought about a change in digital engagement. With a distinctive combination of being both easy to use and having great editing features and quality, it has become one of the most significant forces in modern social media. For those looking to tap into its potential, this critical capability-to know what TikTok is all about and how it works, is the vital first step for thriving in its dynamic and ever-evolving ecosystem.

1.2. How TikTok Works

TikTok is both simple and craftily complex in its design and operation, hence producing an addictive experience for a user. The centerpiece is the Natural "For You" feed, which is natural and personalized based on the unique interests and actions of individuals. So with this, as you open the app, you're plunged head-first into an immediate flow of videos that, in most situations, instantly captivate your attention: some funny comedy skit, lovely dance routine, or helpful tutorial.

The TikTok content creation process is deliberately organized to be very user-friendly. Users can directly shoot their videos in the app and use various editing features to trim speed or slow footage. TikTok users are availed with a giant library of music and sound effects, making it so easy to incorporate popular tunes or originality in the videos of their choice. What is more, the variety of filters and effects on this platform is grasping. It goes from a simple color correction gradient to dazzling augmented reality, which is laid over videos to make creative injections.

TikTok's algorithm is the secret weapon driving the platform. The system applies machine learning algorithms and artificial intelligence to scan user engagement. For example, what videos users watched till the end or what they liked and then shared or commented on.

All of this data is subsequently used to predict the other types of content that the user will enjoy, constantly refining recommendations apparent on the "For You" page. As such, even a person without a single follower might have thousands of people view their video if it resonates with viewers and the algorithm thereof. Another core feature contributing to the participatory and community orientation that is highly identified on TikTok is these trending challenges. Meanwhile, constantly trending hashtag campaigns on the application help in kindling participation. Most of these trends, of course, come from popular creators or brands, while users join in to create their dance, lip-sync, or memes. This would not only help grow such solid communities but subsequently build into the virality of the content, as these users are inspired and continuously grasp someone else's idea.

Going through TikTok's natural user interface is relatively straightforward. There are two primary feeds seen when first reaching the Home screen: "Following" and "For You." The "Following" feed pertains to the accounts a user's friends post, while the content in the "For You" section has recently gained popular favor. Tapping into the various other tabs would render the trending hashtags on the "Discover " page, account notifications on "Inbox," and, after that, individual settings of the user's own. This minimalist design, therefore, implies that users can find and interact with content that is in their best interest very quickly, thus making using TikTok very enjoyable and very engaging.

1.3. Key features and functionalities

The presence of these features and functionalities is thus exciting to use during the creation process and intriguing to explore during the exploration time. The richness of the sound and music library available on TikTok is central to its appeal. This allows users to quickly interject such popular songs, trending audio clips, and even original sounds into their videos, creating a brilliant and dynamic soundtrack attached to their content. In a word, this is an integral part of incorporating music into the addiction of TikTok videos.

The most prominent of such features is the toolkit for video editing right within TikTok. This means that if you have the application, you can shoot right within the application or upload a pre-recorded raw movie and just cut, speed up, slow it down, or split it into multiple pieces.

And let's not forget transitions, filters, and effects—TikTok offers tons of editing tools to give your videos a pro look. Sure, it sounds fancy, but it's easy enough that anyone can do it. From simple color tweaks to mind-blowing AR magic, TikTok has everything you need to make your videos stand out and look awesome. The program suggests thousands of filters and effects, which could turn any application video into a bright and funny spectacular video. The provisions regarding beauty filters, green background removal, and animative effects can be put in to interact with the movements. These provisions augment both the video quality and furnish an enormous scope for the users to unleash ideas suggested over the platform.

The platform enjoys trends and challenges, part of its viral nature. Users can participate in trending challenges by replicating the same dances as lip-syncs or other popular activities. Most of such trends come with specified hashtags, making it very easy for a user to find and take part in. When the user manages to do that, he gets noticed, and he interacts with a broader base of viewers who react to that move by following them and engaging with their posts.

Hashtags and discovery features are essential for content discovery on the platform. The features of the Discover page present the utmost trending hashtags and popular sounds in conjunction with emerging trends so that people are informed about what is hot on the platform.

At its core, hashtags categorize content within the app. In turn, the hashtagging of a post makes a piece of content commercially sustainable, reaching a wider audience—people not following you who can be very significant. That being the case, when content creators apply well and frequently used hashtags, they can get into broader conversations and hold a more significant chance of going viral.

Finally, the analytics provided by TikTok helps creators and commercial brands determine the best content strategy. These tools also provide in-depth metrics on how videos are performing, audience demographics, and engagement rates.

This way, users can understand what types of content are really in line with their audience and adjust these strategies and decisions. Such an approach is crucial in leading creators and brands to the effective growth of their presence on the platform.

In other words, the facilities and features that TikTok comes with are created in a manner that might make the whole process of content generation easy, fun, and very engaging. With its massive music collection and advanced editing tools, combined with its collaborative ingredients and all-embracing statistics, TikTok gives its consumers all the means necessary to put out riveting content in the most robust possible manner.

This is precisely why TikTok emerges as more of a powerhouse amidst the scenario of social media, combining creativity, community, and insights by data.

Key features concerning all this regard include adding sounds and music, effects, filters, effects, and AR effects through duets, stitching, trending hashtags, and challenges. The features on duets and stitching in TikTok offer options to create a few videos out of a single video, as one can copy some parts to interact with such material.

The intuitive, user-friendly interfaces make this platform manageable for users of all kinds—both the old and the young, tech-savvy or not. Upon opening the application, a "For You" page appears. These are fragments or perhaps curated feeds to feed your interests and interactions with videos.

This is the lifeline that makes TikTok impossibly engaging because you can just go on an infinite scroll of a zillion features of tons of content shared on the homepage. It presents users with another video just by swiping up, which is a fluid and uninterrupted surfing experience that leads almost automatically to further watching.

Except for the "For You" page, there are several other essential tabs in the app that help to explore the types of content and modes of interaction venturing. The "Following" tab, located right beside the "For You" tab, posts what the subscribed-to accounts share, which means a person always stays in the know on everything their favorite creators are coming up with.

The next feature is "Discover," marked with an icon of a magnifying glass. It allows users to find trending hashtags, sick beats, and viral challenges and, therefore, stay up to date with trends.

All the content on TikTok is created with the central "Create" button, which is a plus symbol located at the bottom of the screen. This button launches the camera interface where you can record new videos or upload pre-existing ones.

By experience, this field is overly filled with a breadth of tools and options, from a selection of music, speed, and timers to an exhaustive offer of various effects and filters, among others. All of these are pretty readily accessible in use, due to which even the simplest of video recordings prove to be very responsive and relatively high in quality.

It's called the "Inbox" tab, right? Here comes all the information: your likes, comments, new followers, and mentions—the envelope-like icon sends you information thus far. Here, people can send direct messages to you, while simultaneously, you can contact them. Contact management from a single source, contact with the audience—isn't that the magic formula for community building around your online collection?

The person icon behind you could be the "Profile" tab, under which the user controls all the personal account management features. Here, you'll get an option to view your videos, edit your profile information, access settings, and so much more.

A user can add a profile picture, bio, and link to other social media handles or sites on their profile. That makes the profile page a part of TikTok branding and personalization that helps create a memorable impression on anyone visiting your page. Understanding the interface is critical for effective leveraging.

The primary tabs consist of the "Home" feed, "Discover" page, "Create" button, "Inbox" below to use for replies and inbounds, and "Me," where you can further personalize your profile. Learn what role each tab exactly plays in navigating TikTok more easily

CHAPTER 2

Lay the Foundation for Success

One must view Setting Up for Success as setting up the foundation of your TikTok empire for your reign to begin with a final bang, along with maybe a few of those dance moves.

First, your trusty advisors shall guide you in every leg of this journey, starting with creating a TikTok account and selecting the right kind of username to suit one of a digital monarch. But we're not entirely leaving a would-be ruler hopeless, for in this book, we've also unveiled the secret of profile optimization to make any ordinary profile one of the shining stars of TikTok awesomeness.

The visuals would be so jaw-dropping that even the cool cats among them would be left whispering a double take. Not to mention, of course, your follow-your loyal subjects! In the end, by magic, if not by TikTok analytics, we will provide you with what it takes to discern those wants and needs so that your content can be king in their hearts and minds.

Finally, to top it all off, we'll set goals because what monarch doesn't need a little roadmap to TikTok domination? So, grab that scepter—or just your phone—and go on this epic TikTok quest with me!

2.1. Creating Your TikTok Account

The opportunity being created here by making an account on TikTok will most likely be integrated with its limitless potential for branding personal images, creative expressions, or sharing engagement. It is indeed simple; within minutes, you can go into the app and start uploading content.

First, you need to download TikTok from your device's app store. After downloading and installing, the app is launched, and you will see the sign-up or log-in option.

Registration on TikTok is flexible in several ways—whichever has the most appeal for you. You can register by your email address, your phone number, or an already existing social media account via Facebook, Google, or Twitter.

You will have your social media accounts connected to TikTok, making it easy to log in and quickly reach the friends and followers you have elsewhere. You choose your favorite sign-up method, and then, depending on the one you picked, you will be asked to give some basic information and to invent a password.

Coming up with a great TikTok username is a pretty big decision when setting up your account. A username is an identity by which one is known on the platform, forming a big part of your brand identity.

It should be memorable, related to some part of your brand or personal identity, and, in the best possible scenario, similar to other social media usernames. Consistency helps in building a cohesive online presence and makes it easier for your audience to find and follow you across different platforms. Once you've selected an available username, you can move on to customizing your profile.

Personalizing your account can only help you. Start with a high-quality profile picture that best describes you or your brand in the best light. This could be your professional photo, a logo, or an image that best suits you. Then there is a bio, a very short and attractive description of you and the kind of posts. Putting your bio can be seen as one sure way of attracting real potential followers in that they get to know a preview of who you are and the advantages of following you that they would enjoy. Moreover, TikTok also allows you to include links to your websites or any other social profile socials; surely, there will be a way your followers can reach out outside this application.

Look through all that the app offers, from settings to privacy. With TikTok, you can set who you want to view your stuff, who can comment on your videos, and even who can message or mention you.

These preferences, as indicated by your comfort level, can be set up to allow for positive and safe interaction on TikTok as you start. With the setup in the account and full customization in the profile done now, you are ready to go and take a deep dive into the world of TikTok, get creative, and gain an audience worldwide.

In synopsis, it's all simple: first, download the TikTok app from the app store and create an account. Sign up using your email address, phone number, or social media account. Select an appealing profile username relating to your brand that is easy to remember.

2.2 Optimizing your Profile

An optimized TikTok profile is important to leave an impression and garner followers as and when someone stumbles upon your account. It's a window people will look toward and understand who you are and what you, as a creator, will bring to the TikTok community.

To start with optimization, the first aspect is an attractive profile picture portraying your brand or personal identity. Whether that be a spiffy headshot of you or your brand logo, or even a high-quality and engaging image, your profile picture should catch the eye and stick in the audience's mind.

Linking your TikTok to other social media accounts or your website enables the off-flow of one's online presence and channels that flow to all the different sites. In your bio, you convert that not-easily-tapped fan of linking up elsewhere by adding any clickable link, thus encouraging more engagements and participation out of TikTok. Select a link that sends followers to your most relevant or valued content, be it the latest YouTube vlog or an e-commerce shop page.

Make sure to maintain consistency with your TikTok profile and branding. Your username should be relatable or consistent, and your profile picture, along with your bio, should be somewhat similar to any of your other social media. That helps to make recognition easy from followers and for followers to remember you easily.

It will also portray enough credibility since it is pretty uniform or consistent through and through. That said, aspects of your brand visual identity and any other means to solidify brand recognition could be incorporated into the TikTok profile.

Continuous posting of fresh videos, hashtag challenges, and catchy captions will keep your profile relevant and, of course, exciting to your audience. The TikTok algorithm looks at the number of active and engaging accounts; suitable materials posted daily would always ensure excellent visibility, hence a growing number of followers.

You must be versatile in content, style, and topics to keep your account interesting to different audiences.

Moreover, it is essential to establish a great rapport with your audience so that they feel a sense of community around your content. You should reply to comments, messages, and mentions to give your followers appreciation and a sense of belonging. Asking questions, doing Q&As, and hosting polls to elicit responses is an easy way to encourage interaction. Of course, when you pick a Mega relationship between you and your audience, things will increase for good, such as loyalty and engagement, which eventually will grow your TikTok organically.

Your profile is the first impression behind your brand. High-quality image, nice bio, and do not forget to add the links to your website or social profiles. Cover the essence of branding for higher exposure and resiliency.

2.3. Understanding Your Audience

Understanding your target audience is the cornerstone of fulfillment on TikTok and is important for tailoring your content to resonate together with your target demographic. Start by studying TikTok's integrated analytics equipment, which provides treasured insights into your audience's demographics, behavior, and alternatives. This equipment offers information on metrics including age, gender, religion, and interests, allowing you to benefit from a deeper knowledge of who your followers are and what content material they revel in.

Pay interest in your followers' engagement styles, including when they are most lively on the platform and which kinds of content they have interacted with the most.

These records will let you optimize your posting schedule to reach your target audience while they may be most likely to be online and receptive to your content. Additionally, perceive tendencies or ordinary issues in your maximum famous films to discover what resonates most together with your audience.

Engage together with your target market without delay through comments, messages, and polls to acquire feedback and insights into their options and interests.

Encourage them to share their thoughts, reviews, and tips for future content, and pay attention attentively to their remarks. Building a dialogue with your audience now not best fosters a feel of the network but also presents treasured insights that can inform your content strategy and help you better serve your target market's wishes.

To go a step further, use the features that are available in TikTok such as the moment polls, Q&A, and live audio to get feedback from the audience in a more engaging way.

These features not only motivate people to participate but also allow for engaging with the audience on a higher level and further foster the development of a targeted relationship. But, use them wisely to get a better understanding of your audience's needs, hobbies as well as their attitude towards different issues.

Audience analysis and, more specifically, the monitoring of the patterns within a given niche or industry can also help one gain a wealth of information about the audience. Follow trends such as hashtags, challenges, and going viral to keep up with trendy content that will work for your audience.

Thus, it is possible to keep following the main trends which will enable the definition of the most efficient content strategy as far as the target audience is concerned.

Furthermore, make sure you are aware of the fact that the identification of the audience and the recognition of its needs is not an ultimate goal that can be attained once and for all but a process that needs to be carried out repeatedly and constantly, with all the results obtained is subject to further analysis and improvement.

Generate new content that is interesting and relevant to its target market and do not limit yourself to a specific format, topic, or style. Therefore, it is always useful to pay attention to your audience, receive their feedback, and adapt your strategy based on it, as this will help to establish trust within the TikTok community and ensure that your audience helps further the development of your brand on the platform.

2.4. Setting Clear Goals

Several people head to TikTok just to make a few comedy videos, sing along to their favorite songs or dance in front of the camera before they set their goal on the platform. Do you have the desire to become the Next Big Thing that will go 'viral,' or the probabilities of this are almost as likely as hitting the jackpot? Therefore, it is relevant to set realistic objectives depending on the available resources, some professional success, and market targeting.

When getting on various platforms it is very common to set targets such as the number of followers, the level at which individuals will engage with the content posted, or how many leads can be generated for the business, having achievable objectives will ensure that you are not discouraged in the process and also ensure that you can determine the extent of your success.

To make goals more tangible, some rules can be followed: After you define the goals, divide them by objectives that are easier to measure.

Whether you're starting or seeking to enhance your TikTok presence, consider them as mini-missions along the way to the ultimate goal. For instance, if you are focusing on raising brand awareness, the specific action plans that you may follow may include developing content schedules and engaging in regular posts and responses.

This means that you will have to make the goals feel less like big spoons of medicine that nobody wants to take and more like small biscuits that have to be eaten one at a time.

Ensure that set goals are Specific, Measurable, Attainable, Relevant, and Time-bound or what is commonly known as SMART goals.

This string of letters might bring to mind a new-age workshop, but in reality, it is rather helpful and accurate when it comes to goal setting. For example, instead of saying 'I want to get more followers', you set your goals in a SMART manner such as 'I wish to get 20% more followers within the next 3 months'. In this manner, at least you have a firm direction as well as a preferable time constraint in place.

Remember to have fun with your goals, this is TikTok we are dealing with not some corporate meeting.

I had a great learning experience when it comes to goal setting and that is never stick to objectives that are ordinary and common, one must set goals that are fun and challenging. Perhaps, you wish to set a goal that would be exciting to accomplish, such as to develop the dance trend of the year or work with a specific TikTok star. The sky's the limit must be the dream of the heart and don't let anyone dull that passion of yours.

Remember as you strive towards your goal the plan sometimes has to change slightly. Instagram is ever-changing, and what can be successful now may not be in the foreseeable future.

Be willing and ready to experiment with adapting new strategies or taking tactics that may flatten you out. Just remember, everything is a part of the story and the journey, so just get down that winding road and you'll come out on the other side more prepared for the bumps in the road.

Finally, be sure to do so along the way, that is, to take time and celebrate the achievements made. It could be the mark you hit on the followers' count if your video is included in the "For You " tab or if you receive a compliment or appreciation from your fans, do not underestimate the power of congratulating yourself.

You have done your best to reach your goal, and deserve to be proud of yourself and the results you have achieved. Well, come on, life is too short to be too serious, so put your dancing shoes on and just let your funny bone show on your TikTok videos!

CHAPTER 3

Building Interesting Narrative

This is where the fun part begins for your TikTok marketing adventure in the Crafting Engaging Content section. We will explain the multitude of content that can be created; from lip-sync videos to funny sketches; providing you the incentive to be stupid and silly (which is quite good for you sometimes, as you might discover new talents you possess).

We will also discuss what's up with jumping onto trends and challenges, come on, who doesn't like dancing to the new trend or meme challenge? Moreover, examples of storytelling that will help you engage your listeners from start to finish – a brief on how to be the Spielberg of TikTok.

What is worth mentioning; is the clear and great visuals, together with great-sounding music to which it is worth admitting that on Tik Tok it is worth focusing on the factor *wow*. So gear up to solve everyone's midnight munchies by supplying information that is as irresistible as a bag of chips.

3.1. Content Types on TikTok

In any case, what I've come to learn when it comes to creating good content with TikTok is that the more diverse the reel, the more appealing it is to Gen Z.

Many people think that TikTok provides a variety of different content categories to select from, and it is very appetizing to choose from that smorgasbord. Whether you are into pop videos, dancing comedy or educational videos then TikTok has something for you.

There are many kinds of accounts, but the most frequently used one is the lip-sync video that appears on TikTok. This format enables the users to sing along to their favorite songs or record themselves speaking the lines of their favorite movies or any funny audio they find interesting.

The lip-sync videos may be as simple as shooting a video of someone performing the lyrics of a song and are fun, simple, and popular among beginners and experts in the TikTok application.

Another type of content that wouldn't be out of place on TikTok is Dance challenges; try telling that to the people who find themselves creating it in front of a camera. From funny dance challenges such as the "Renegade" dance to contemporary choreographed dances set to trending popular songs, dancing also forms an excellent way of self-expression as well as a method of connecting with other people. Furthermore, they are a good opportunity to have a walk and to free oneself from the magnificent weight of quarantine snacks.

If you think you have a funny bone in you then TikTok should be your go-to place and launch-pad to the world of comedy and humor. Comedy has recently become one of the most watched genres by TikTok users where short yet funny sketches, skits, and memes are expected from the funny TikTok users.

Even though it mimics current trends or creates humor out of the most ordinary life occurrences, comedy content is a sure path to cheer up someone and also make one or two jokes out of it.

It also encompasses instructional content because people perform tutorials, teaching guides, informative videos and live streams. It can include recipes, home improvement insights, language courses, instructions, scientific discoveries, and many other topics that will be helpful to users who want to acquire new knowledge or improve certain skills. Also, it is very effective and popular to define yourself as a specialist in your field and attract like-minded people to you.

Another format in TikTok is the possibility of telling stories as users can upload a speech or simply share a story with their audience regarding their experience in life. From a joke overheard, to a day in someone's life, a success story or a drug addiction story, storytelling videos, therefore, can touch base with the audience and bring out a feeling of oneness.

Music videos/montages are one of the most frequent themes among the users who have decided to express their creativity and perform arts.

With music videos, you can make an artistic statement of your creativity and technical skills especially when you are editing the scenes in conjunction with the rhythm of your preferred music tune whether you are making a movie montage or a montage of your travels, among other occasions. Also, it is effective since they are interactive and can pass your interests and hobbies to the audience easily.

One can suggest the use of the combination of the mentioned content forms and the use of appropriate combinations or 'con litigation' of such forms. Do not limit yourself to one format, one style or one theme; be creative to produce your content. Of course, TikTok is all about creativity and freedom, so don't be shy, and don't keep to the canons, simply create something new.

No matter whether you want to combine comedy and dance education and entertainment, or music and tale, TikTok gives you freedom. So have fun and paint the town red man; you can never overdo it if only the limit is your imagination.

3.2. Trends and Challenges

Creativity and growth cannot be sustained without trends and challenges, thus trends and challenges are the life of TikTok. Now about the trends, the most significant aspect of TikTok, there is virtually no idea that would be implemented repeatedly, giving the audience an endless list of ideas. Being current is important to both feed your content sources as well as keep your audience interested in what you know and share with them.

If there is one aspect that immediately defines TikTok it is the way it can take any song, dance, or meme and spread it around the world within days. However, dances are one of the most popular trends that are associated with the use of TikTok where individuals across the globe cannot wait to follow the trends and join the fervor of dances.

Starting from the "WAP" dance to the "Savage" challenge, viral dances are often a great way of involving your target audience and being a part of the TikTok community.

Apart from viral dances, TikTok contains different hashtag challenges which means that the users should perform something unusually and interestingly.

From challenges related to cooking, and painting houses to dancing or lip-syncing, hashtags are an excellent tool in trying to make people be creative and unite. Also using hashtags in the challenges you take can increase your visibility and get people visiting your page, looking for content from the challenge.

The "For You" page and the Discover tab tell users what is new and hot in the app; thus, it is useful to regularly monitor them to get an understanding of the tendencies and difficulties on TikTok.

These parts of the app demonstrate popular videos, hashtags, and challenges, which gives creators a goldmine of ideas to work with. They should be visited often as they will help one identify new trends before they get popular and hence exploit them.

That is why cooperation with other authors is another good tool to use TikTok trends and challenges in your account to boost your audience and engagement.

By constructing your account and collaborating with other similar users you can reach out to other people from a similar niche and their followers. Whether it is a duet, Stitch or joint challenge, collaborations are good ways of working with other creators and therefore growing your audience on TikTok.

You should not be shy to dance to your style, the different trends and challenges you post should in some way be your flavor or that of your brand. Whether it be in dancing and creating a dance like this or in incorporating a new funny hashtag challenge into a video, the more you add your personality to it, the more you are likely to draw the attention of many people towards your account. Anyway, the main idea of TikTok is a platform where everyone is free to be creative, so let your imagination unchain and come up with unique ways of performing the trends or doing the challenges.

3.3. Storytelling Techniques

Telling a story on TikTok is as complex as telling an enthralling story that could be told in a minute, a minute and a half at most – but where there is a great reward in it. Whether you are telling a joke or telling a life story, or when you want to pass a message, a good one will make your stay glued to their ears.

To master the art of storytelling on TikTok, consider incorporating the following techniques into your content:

Mainly, attracts the viewers' attention from the start of the video. With millions of videos to choose from, you have 5 seconds to grab the attention and make the viewers bang on the like button and continue watching. To capture the reader's attention begin with a mini-thesis statement, pose a question, show a clip or tell a story. Whichever of the hooking techniques you decide to go for – a musical one, a twist, or a powerful visualization, ensure that at the very least, your first shot does the trick and keeps the audience glued to the rest of the narration.

To retain such attention, the mode of presenting information has to be coherent, straightforward and follow a logical pattern of informative narration. All good narratives have a start, middle, and end; the same applies to the now-famous TikTok videos.

Getting started simply means outlining the setting, or what background a particular story has. Who are the characters? What is the setting? What is the weakness or problem that they encounter? Entice the audience to watch your video through pictures, speech, and story.

In the remaining part of your story ensure that you focus on the tense and suspense to make your viewers engage. Most viewers like to be engaged by subsequent events that are best introduced in terms of obstacles, conflict or challenges that characters have to face to progress along the plotline. It is always recommended to make the narrative dramatic by using such features as cliffhangers, plot twists and build-up surprises. Do not forget that the major idea of narration is to maintain viewers' interest and their desire to see the story's continuation.

It pays to include aspects of funniness, feelings or drama into your work to make it easier for people to be touched. Humor, pathos, and suspense are the main tools of an amusing audience; in any case, an emotional reaction is an important means of achieving the goal of great narration.

Comedic to make it less serious or appeal to viewers' emotions to let them identify with the material or employ unconstructive suspense to make the audience wait till the last possible second.

It is also important that one should not forget the important aspects such as pacing and rhythm of the story. TikTok videos are short and can often last for a few seconds. Once the main idea is expressed, it is important to move on.

Make sure you do not slow the activity by taking too much time to explain things that do not warrant explanation or by wandering off-topic. Add zoom-ins and outs, wipes, dissolves and effects to prevent viewers from getting bored and to sustain their interest from beginning to end. Of course, everyone knows that short and sweet is the name of the game when it comes to TikTok.

Moreover, make sure to wrap up the story in a way that will end the film on a high note and will make people leave the cinema satisfied. You might also need to provide a nice wrap-up of outstanding issues, wrap up a conflict that remained open during your presentation or leave your audience with a strong call to action statement.

You must always ask yourself if the ending of your story is strong and memorable and how it supports the whole point of the story. However, the best things in a cinematic production are usually the ones that linger in the audience's mind even after the picture has made its final roll.

3.4. Tips for Captivating Visuals

Creating catchy thumbnails for the TikTok content can be best compared to cooking a delicious meal; in this case, it will be necessary to add a pinch of inspiration a few drops of talent, and, of course, a large portion of passion. When more than 500 million hours of videos are uploaded to the platform daily, it is critical to make your content pretty and easy to remember. Here are some tips to help you whip up visually stunning TikTok videos that will leave your audience hungry for more:

Ok first things first, let's have light! Lighting is this special ingredient in how your videos look so appetizing that people would want to take a bite. Your best ally is light so if you can do it, try to shoot near the window in the daytime. But if you end up shooting in the dark, do now worry – just go to some store and buy cheap light equipment to illuminate your star – which is you.

Choosing the composition is all about considering your video to be a canvas that is yet to be created. Question the set and environment and move around to get various positions, views and approaches to a shot. Try something new, and do not be confined within the frame – Picasso did not paint within the frame, and you should not as well.

Nothing brings life into a video more than colors; it is time to spice up your TikTok videos. Spice up the content and make it eye-popping and inviting with bright hues, or you can make it lean back, and taste with hushed tones. You do not necessarily have to be a fan of the rainbow or a master of monochromaticity; do not be scared to go crazy to get your viewers' vision satisfied.

You should spice up your videos a little and include something as action to make your audience more active. Movement enhances the show factor in any content type, ranging from splendid leg operations to perfect shots. Well, rock and roll and get as wild as you would like just don't stain the sauce!

Details, darling, details! When you're in front of the camera, consider details such as costumes, props, and things within the set as a way of offering your audience delicious imagery. After all, the addition would be more important because they are garnishing the dish so do not be thrifty.

Oh, and no video can go wrong without the chopped and changed magic that TikTok has to offer. With filters, stickers, and music to transition, TikTok has a buffet of tools that can be used to enhance the appeal of the content. Just be careful not to go gaga – you do not wish your video to be a complete mess!

Do not forget about the final piece of advice – do not betray your individualistic taste. However, this is where people should remember what sets them apart and remain relevant to the current trends out there.

Add your flavour, style and attitude to the videos along with your comedic side to make the dish that is you. Of course, nobody knows that the best juices, salads, and soups are prepared with the addition of love and, if possible, a pinch of humor!

3.5. Effective Use of Music and Sounds

Bravo, bravo – quite literally, thank you TikTok, for being our ears for once. To master the use of music and sound in TikTok is all about harmonizing creativity just like the notes of a melody.

Whether singing along to today's popular song or disturbing a cheesy comedy play with appropriate noises, using the right music and sounds can turn a plain TikTok video into one of the best. So, let's tune in and discover how to hit all the right notes: So, let's tune in and discover how to hit all the right notes:

First things first, your soundtrack selection should be carefully made. Just as finding the right cheese for your pizza, the right kind of music can either make or mar a TikTok video. If you decide to use such things as pop songs harmonies of famous movies, or something that can hardly be heard by anyone, make sure that all this fits the content and mood. Besides, one wouldn't serve up a Metallica track when people are coming over for a cup of tea unless perhaps it was a Metallica Tea Party.

After that, try to diversify your often boring choice of sound effects. It seems that TikTok has every possible sound imaginable from every laugh, every animal, every skit, and every cartoon box you can think of. Therefore, feel free to combine sounds to become the author of the individual audio composition. Wait, what if one day you find out that loud sound of a fart is exactly what is missing in your comedy sketch?

Thus, the point here is that while moving with music, the most crucial thing is not the choice of steps. The strategy of moving in harmony with the music is rather useful, just like when the dancers perform their spectacular show. Lip singing or dancing, ensure that your actions are well synchronized with the actions in the song. Indeed, no one would be interested in a TikTok dance, which is even more clumsy than a drummer with two left feet!

Don't neglect the volume – no one wants a loud next door, or in this case, on TikTok. Ensure that your music and your sound are fine-tuned so that they enhance the content of what you are presenting without dominating it. Who seeks to hear your great punch-line or your slaps of witty dialogue? Does he get that or is he dismissed by an irritating sound?

Expand the choices of music selection and try out different genres and styles of music for chosen videos. As different as hip-hop, country, edam and of course classical are there is always music that fits your preferences on TikTok.

Therefore, one should not be shy and succumb to the constraints of personal musical preferences – it can be useful to finally turn to 'the dark corner' and hear the songs that you normally would not listen to.

Importantly, do not forget to be as creative as you can when drawing these diagrams and also have fun.

TikTok is the new generation app for creativity, to express oneself, and for entertainment. Hence, do not hold back and be yourself; dance crazily, and sing to the karaoke tunes like a star, even if one is wearing pajamas. Anyway, the world is way too serious to be too serious about oneself – so turn the volume up high, press the play button, and dance to the melodies setting off on a TikTok journey!

CHAPTER 4

The Power of Hashtags and Captions

In this chapter, we'll explore the importance of hashtags and captions on TikTok. Hashtags can help your videos get noticed and even go viral. We'll show you how to find and use the best hashtags to get your videos on the "For You" page.

You'll learn about trending hashtags and more specific ones that can increase your post's visibility and engagement. Grab your hashtag skills and let's conquer TikTok together. Who knows, maybe a simple #ReDovideos hashtag will make you the next big thing on TikTok!

4.1 Choosing the right hashtags

Oh yes, the small and simple #hashtag – what are these small signs doing on such a fabulous platform as TikTok? Hashtags are the seasonings in your content and picking the right one can change the way people perceive your content in the same way that a good seasoning can change the taste of a dish.

They can make the difference between a video seen by 10 people and one that goes viral. Again, think of them like planting seeds in a garden—plant the right hashtags, and watch your content grow and spread to the perfect audience. Let's dive into how you can use hashtags to boost your TikTok fame

Before you start creating on TikTok, it's essential to do some research! Like a chef picking the best ingredients, take time to explore the trending hashtags in your niche. Visit the "Discover" tab, check out similar creators, and see what's currently trending. Look for hashtags that are popular and relevant to your content and target audience.

This way, you'll know which hashtags to use to maximize your video's reach and engagement.

It needs to be noted that there should be a balanced approach when choosing hashtags, the ones that are general and can be used in various posts, and the ones that are specific to a certain topic. Just like sprinkling salt on your dish, using a combination of popular and specific hashtags makes your content be seen by many while at the same time having a targeted audience.

Therefore, use the very common 'popular' hashtags to reach many people and also incorporate the 'specific' niche relevant hashtags to reach people who are specifically interested in that niche.

Popular tags like #fyp and #viral can quickly get your content in front of thousands, if not millions, of users, but the competition is fierce. Balance these with specific hashtags related to your content to target a more focused audience. For instance, if you're posting a cooking video, use general hashtags like #cooking along with niche tags like #veganrecipes or #quickmeals. This way, you reach both a broad and a targeted audience.

On this note, the size of the hashtag pool should also come into consideration. Just like when selecting between a tiny children's pool and a large Olympic pool, if you engage with hashtags, that are not used by many other people, your photos are likely to be noticed by a large number of people. That way largely, frequently used hashtags may seem very attractive but are very saturated with the result of your post being buried somewhere in the search.

Therefore, it is recommended that you do not disregard checking the less popular hashtags – maybe here you will find something that will turn your content into a real viral sensation.

It is also important to track relevant trends and topics in current events to use hot tags straight away. Similar to changing up your seasonal specials, including timely hashtags can make the content you put out feel timely and relevant.

Whether it is a hashtag challenge, something amusing to Williams, or a current event, including a trending hashtag can help increase the visibility and interaction that a specific post will receive. So, check out the Discover page to see what's trending and use those hashtags. The only thing you should avoid is adding yourself to the wrong hashes simply because they are trending; people do not like those who try to take advantage of any trend related to their topic to gain traffic.

Also, consider creating your own branded hashtags. Encourage your followers to use these tags when posting related content. For example, a fitness influencer could create a hashtag like

#FitnessWithAnna, and followers can use it to share their workout sessions.

This not only boosts your exposure but also adds credibility to your brand. Always remember that there are no fixed rules regarding hashtag use so you can experiment all you want. Just as when people use fancy spices in the kitchen, to make the content distinctive and grab the audience's attention, one should employ unusual and bright hashtags.

While it is possible to create hashtags right from the name of the organization or the product, don't be afraid to be creative and come up with hashtags that would fit your brand's personality and tone.

After all, some imagination can go a long way in ensuring that your content is quite easy to share with others.
Use the hashtags in different combinations to know which of them will suit your content. This is in the same way that one tests their ingredients in a recipe book by trying different tastes in combination with each other, an experiment can be done with hashtags to find the best one.

Remember which hashtags are popular with the content you post and change how you do it if it is not successful.

As with the choice of hashtags, it is significant to know that it is not universal to follow a specific strategy, which has proven effective for someone else, but may not always be effective for someone else, so do not hesitate to try different things. While doing this, note that you can use up to ten hashtags but on TikTok, the allowed maximum is 100 characters.

Not all hashtags will be effective, so it's important to analyze which ones bring the most likes and engagement. In other words, be mindful of the diminishing results as measured by views, likes, comments, and shares to assess your success of the hashtag campaign and optimize it if necessary. Regularly check your metrics to refine your strategy and maximize your reach. And don't be afraid to experiment with new hashtag combinations.

TikTok trends change rapidly, so stay flexible and keep testing new ideas to keep your content fresh and discoverable. Remember, the goal is to make your content as searchable and engaging as possible using the best hashtags.

4.2. Crafting Engaging Captions

Oh, the beauty of captions!!! – that simple set of words that you need to select, to take your ordinary TikTok video and turn it into an extraordinary one. Choosing good captions is always like deploying the cherry on the cake; it makes the meal even sweeter and attractive and makes the content even more alluring. Here is the guide to capture captions and learn how to make the ones that will dazzle your audience and make them laugh out loud.

First of all, you must define your audience. Similar to how an efficient chef gets acquainted with his clientele's manners and food choices, you have to comprehend who your viewers are, and what they appreciate. Are there funny posts, motivational posts, or informative posts or does it contain something completely different?

Adapt the captions to their profiles and personality. Good humor could be a clever joke which might be funny for a young group while the same might be impressed by a philosophical quote in a senior group.

Following that, make the statement short but memorable. Given that TikTok is a social media platform with reprimanded video production, conciseness is vital.

Just as the appetizer should be perfectly sized to whet your appetite it is often the same for your caption. It is recommended to be laconic and use strong words; do not get distracted by long descriptions that may lead to the audience's disinterest. Do not forget that the viewers watch hundreds of videos per day, and your video should attract their attention at once with a brilliant caption.

The use of call-to-action (CTA) could also be used in the marketing strategies. The caption is more or less like having an open conversation with the potential viewers and engaging them with the material you post.

No matter whether you post the question, encourage people to comment, or encourage them to participate in the challenge, a proper CTA can skyrocket the engagement. For instance, a caption such as 'What do you like to do in summer? Leave your comments below!' not only incites your audience to leave comments but also your video likely gets more views and also gets to be shared on more social media channels.

Humour is your friend. Similar to adding some salt to a sweet dish, adding a bit of humor to your caption will make it more informal and thus more likely to be liked and shared.

You do not have to be formal and it would sometimes be good to make your audience crack a smile. It has been seen that a simple pun or a joke that may be considered funny gets the viewer on the right side instantly. But always be careful not to go overboard on the jokes, and especially do not try to reduce your audience to tears in case you are creating sensitive jokes.

Applying emojis to your messages – This is a way of making your messages more interesting and also as a way of passing an emotion about a certain topic or issue. Generally, emojis are like the spice rack where you can get flavor, color or even emphasis to your captions. However, similar to spice moderation should be observed. While several emojis are visually appealing in a caption, it can make the caption extremely congested as well.

They're perfect to underline certain points in the caption, share your mood, or make the caption funnier. For example, a brief caption such as "Feeling fabulous today" or "All smiles today, " accompanied by a happy emoji will inform followers about the positive mood.

Ensure that you are using the modern words that are often used in everyday conversation. Similar to these current trends in dishes, it's always relevant to be in tune with current social language to make your captions more interesting.

However, do it organically and make sure that all the phrases you choose are rather relevant to your content and close to your character. Making forced use of popular trends, tags, or especially, slang can be a big put-off among your viewers.

And then lastly, don't be afraid to play and prototype – or fluidly transition to a better method. Similar to baking a cake to the desired recipe, it is not rare to try different captions to find the right one. Focus on which captions are echoing with fans about the content through likes, comments, and shares that the audience provides.

Find out which kinds of captions produce the most responses so that you can be more strategic in your approach. Perhaps, you will detect that the humorous captions bring the most engagement as opposed to questions that bring more engagement in the form of comments. Apply these findings as recommendations for future enhancements of what you offer and how you do so.

In essence, writing a catchy caption is a skill that entails the following: knowing your audience, not being lengthy, using a call to action, enhancing the post with humor, using emojis, adopting trending phrases and experimenting often. Your captions should be thought of as the last touch that enhances the message you have been conveying; making it more interesting, and easier to remember.

Similarly to any beautifully plated dish is served with an equally stunning garnish, so the creative and catchy caption can bring the same effect to the

TikTok video and make it more eye-catching, more likely to be shared and, as a result – more popular. Therefore, it is time to put on the chef's hat and create those enticing captions that are going to ignite the desire of your viewers!

4.3. Analyzing Hashtag Performance

It is highly useful to learn about and assess the performance and effectiveness of hashtags on the TikTok platform to enhance your strategy. Hashtags are not just pretty little additional features; they are effective means that can produce quite a difference in visibility and response. Now, let's review how you can properly evaluate hashtag effectiveness and thus make the most of this strategy.

First, one must make use of TikTok analytics that are available to help in tracking the performance. Thus, by analyzing views and responses that specific content acquires along with likes, shares, and comments, metrics related to particular hashtags can be determined. It is highly useful data to know what can be heard and what cannot be heard by the targeted public.

While assessing the performance of a hashtag, focus on the percentage of engagement. A hashtag that has many views but few people interact with it could be less useful than a less popular hashtag with more people interacting with it. The likes, comments and shares suggest that not only are your posts being viewed, but there is a positive response towards them.

This is a clear depiction that the hashtag brings in active account traffic, meaning the audience you are bringing in deems your content useful and relevant.

The other factor to reflect on is the environment in which the hashtags are being posted. Of them, are they relevant to the content of your video? In the case of hashtags, certain guidelines have to be followed and the most important of them all is the relevance of the hashtag.

If the hashtag is in anyway off the mark, it will draw people who are not interested in your content at all, thus, they are likely to churn. Ideally, the performance of locally appropriate hashtags demonstrates how your content is meeting the expectations of the targeted customers.

In analysing data up to this level and comparing hashtags' performance over time, you can also discover trends and patterns. For instance, you might find out that some hashtags will give better results on certain days or at certain times. Such information is useful for finding the best time to post. Moreover, tracking the season-specific or the event-specific keywords which include hashtags will assist in making the most of the tendencies, thus topical and interesting.

It is also useful to compare your outcome with others or competitors or other people in your particular field. Looking at the hashtags, which the accounts you are monitoring are using, and their performance, you can catch glimpses of successful strategies that you could apply in your content. It is possible to use comparison tools that can be found in various third-party resources such as Social Blade to rectify this situation.

Another important element of evaluating the results of the analyzed hashtag is the experimentation. It is perfectly okay to experiment with a new hashtag or a new combination of the hashtags you'll be using. It can be useful for finding new ways of engagement and development since it is more like experimenting. A method that should be adopted is constantly re-evaluating and creating new and modified hashtags to keep the content relevant and gain new followers.

Lastly, the knowledge acquired from the hashtags' performance will enable the formulation of proper decisions or changes in content. If the use of particular hashtags in the post results in better engagement, then those hashtags should be used often in posts.

On the other hand, if some hashtags are not effective then it is best to opt for better or more prevalent hashtags. Thus, by adjusting your actions repeatedly to the data collected over time, it is easy to keep content growing while achieving sustainable results on TikTok.

Therefore, I learned that hashtag performance analysis is an activity that always means paying attention to the details, and relevancy, and is a must-do activity, geared towards testing and experimenting. By using the analytics of TikTok, knowing the engagement rates and benchmarks, as well as the competitors, and improving the strategy it's possible to make sure that the hashtags that are being used improve the content visibility and engagement. The efficacy of this approach lies in the capacity of data to precisely distinguish what needs to be done to enhance the branding impact of your TikTok profile.

CHAPTER 5

Monetizing Your TikTok Presence

When you're ready to turn your dancing into a paid gig, "Monetizing Your TikTok Presence" is the chapter you need. Ready to dive into TikTok's treasure chest and earn money by being creative? We'll explain how to join this exclusive club and make money doing what you love: Creating great videos.

Think of it as your ticket to the TikTok chocolate factory—where the rewards are for dancing like nobody's watching and creating sketch comedy. So join us on this money-making journey. Your next video could be your ticket to TikTok millionaire status!

5.1. TikTok's Creator Fund

It is not just an idea that you can turn your TikTok following into money but a reality, as TikTok has a Creator Fund. This was introduced primarily to motivate the creators to upload good content that will help them make money depending on the performance of the uploaded videos. The Creator Fund operates on a straightforward principle: That the amount of revenue you can make will increase corresponding to the number of views and interactions in the videos.

In other words, TikTok pays its account based on total views, likes, shares and comments of the videos that are shared by the creators. Being a Creators Fund member normally entails certain conditions that include but not limited to having a depended on minimum limit in number of followers (at least 10,000 followers), abiding to TikTok policies and rules, and having a set volume of views on videos not below a fixed period of time.

As a result, these criteria guarantee the fund's focus on active creators who foster TikTok's enthusiastic community.

When a creator joins the Creator Fund, they get paid based on their video's performance and user location. TikTok shares ad revenue from ads shown with their content and may offer other monetization options in the future. Obviously, joining the Creator

Fund is beneficial as it encourages content creators to consistently produce high-quality content. This transforms TikTok from just an entertainment app, into a potential source of income, allowing creators to invest more time and effort into their videos. As a result, viewers enjoy a greater variety and higher quality of content.

Apart from the monetary aspect, the creation of such content gives the creators an opportunity to use analytics offered by TikTok. Currently, these insights assist viewers to know their audience better, monitor the performance of their videos and navigate on how to design their material to increase on the viewership and ultimately the earnings.

Through these tools, content creators can make better decisions as to the kind of material they wish to produce and/or how they intend to communicate with their audience. In order to engage participation in the Creator Fund, it is necessary to try and find out which type of content will be effective, work with popular topics and challenges, and continue the communication with the audience.

The above analysis of TikTok users' content and audiences reveal that diversification and program adaptation may help boost the probability of obtaining better revenue and stable profitability in the future.

Although the Creator Fund is a massive opportunity to generate money, there are also other ways to make extra money on TikTok. Such as partnering with brands, marketing, selling merchandise or offering subscribers-only content. The following is a combination of two benefits of diversification where it increases the sources of income while these opportunities also help users to get promotions, new job offers, and brand visibility on the application.

In a nut shell, the three observations that would lead to the improved exploitation of earnings from the fund include; consistency in contributing good material, viability in interacting with the followers and an understanding of the policy conducting TikTok.

Therefore, when the basic requirements for a creator are met, they can create interesting content that can help them earn a substantial income based on TikTok's analytics.

5.2. Sponsored Content and Brand Deals

Promotion and partnership on TikTok offer creators many ways to earn money and create unique content for their audience. Influencer marketing for instance, involves collaborations between influencers and brands to promote products or services, making it different from other types of advertising.

There can be no successful sponsored content if the product or service in question is not sincere and genuine in its intention. A content creator works with brands that appeal to their targeted niche, belief system, and the buyers' demographic.

For instance, a fitness influencer can collaborates with a health food business in which they actually use and believe, pushing items that are relevant to their audience's interest in healthy lifestyle. Similarly, a tech reviewer works with a gadget firm whose items they trust and recommend to ensure authenticity and relevancy to their tech-savvy audience.

Such an alignment guarantees that sponsored content appears more organic as well as makes all associated content more trustworthy and credible in the eyes of their followers.

It is very important that there is transparency especially when dealing with organized sponsorships for the content. TikTok also requires the authors to clearly state that the content they produce is sponsored, and thus it is essential for creators to follow the necessary rules of the platform and gain trust of their viewers about the cooperation with the company.

Successful sponsored content goes beyond mere advertising; it's about creators telling stories and showcasing products uniquely. Whether through new narratives, showcasing product benefits, or integrating brands into everyday life, compelling sponsored content engages viewers and encourages active participation.

In reality, you the creator need to know your worth while trying to chat deals involving the sponsored content.

The cost is dependent on factors like the intended audience, reach and participation rates, quality and relevance of content, and targeted specialty areas. Defining essential aspects of a business partnership such as the deliverables, deadlines, and the way of payment and usage, would benefit each participating business.

Originality must be preserved even when collaborating with a sponsor on an advertisement or a brief. What I am trying to tell you is that, when teaming up with a sponsor, keep your originality intact—don't let the brand message cramp your style or alter your values. Staying true to yourself and your creativity makes the ad more authentic and appealing to viewers, which spells success for the brand!

The goal is to "get to the star", hence don't stop at the partnership or sponsorship level, instead, regularly follow and engage with brands. Creators can attract sponsored content and opportunities to become brand ambassadors. Consistently producing high-quality content and maintaining professionalism in projects builds credibility that brands look for when targeting active TikTok users.

Moreover, Tik Tokers should make sure their channel's audience is interested or likely to be interested in what sponsors offer before choosing sponsored content opportunities. Authenticity in promoting brands and products that align with their content and viewership help maintain long-term success on TikTok.

5.3. Marketing Your Own Product or Service

Using TikTok as a marketplace means creators have a global stage to hawk their wares—whether it's physical products, digital goodies, or even educational materials. It's like setting up a lemonade stand in the middle of Times Square!

Hence, it is crucial to target your products or services to the consumers' interest for any sales on the TikTok platform. Knowing the demographic's likes ensures that the product and the promotional materials are what the people want, thus improving the odds of transforming the individuals watching the commercials into clientele.

It is important to note that creativity is a core factor while using TikTok for advertising products or services. Instead of just presenting objects, while you introduce your products to clients, try to paint a picture or showcase how useful your product is.

Stories and examples make the audience interested in continuing the information consumed and are eager to undertake the action. Promote your products or services using TikTok's features in an unconventional approach. Since the medium lends itself well to the use of media and the inclusion of diverse pointers and hints, do not neglect the opportunity to showcase your offerings engagingly using videos, tutorials, customer testaments, and other materials.

It is possible to leverage the TikTok algorithm to build up desire and convey its limitations, ultimately boosting product sales. It is advisable to make special calls to action, such as limited time offers, special promotional prices or offers and special two for one or special offers as a way of getting viewers to purchase.

The calls-to-action in your videos and the captions will leave the customer convinced to buy, making the process seamless. This will go along way in building an effective communication practice since engagement with the target audience is very important.

This comes as something very important in the modern business world where customer relations are of essence. Polite and fast replies to the comments, messages, and inquiries. Solicit the customers for their feedback and testimonials with regard to the consumption of the products or the acquisition of the services being sold in an effort to show the presence of others who have used them successfully.

Another way to cash in on TikTok is by using its selling tools: add web links to your videos directing viewers to your store or use shopping tags for quick access to featured products.

Simplifying the buying process makes it convenient and often triggers impulse purchases. Remember to always track in data by using click-through rates, conversions, and income produced allows you to monitor and measure the efficacy of TikTok campaigns that offer items. Use these information to fine-tune your strategy and increase sales over time.

The key to selling on tiktok means staying true to yourself and being very detailed. Remind your audience about the new products/services, customer testimonies, and enhancements to products to keep them interested and engaged.

Real-world marketing leads to an establishment of a relationship that is credible and therefore increases client traffic and repeat business. Using TikTok, producers may market their work, attract a larger audience, share innovative ideas, interact with viewers, and even offer items or services to interested consumers. TikTok, as a matter of fact, is more than simply a tool for creating content; it can also be used to establish a business and make money.

5.4. Other Monetization Strategies

Apart from the TikTok Creator Fund, sponsored content, and selling your products/services, there are many other monetization strategies that can be used by the content creators to increase their potential earnings on the platform. Affiliate marketing is a popular way to make money by promoting other people's products through special links.

Creators earn a commission for every sale made through these links. For example, a gamer can share an affiliate link for their favorite gaming chair, or a fashion influencer can share a link to trendy clothes, earning a cut from each purchase.

Promoting products like clothes, shoes, gadgets, and more is a common way to make money on TikTok. Along with TikTok Shops and external e-shop links, creators can sell song downloads, ringtones, and merchandise directly in the app. They also earn revenue through brand licensing, which strengthens the brand and community identity. Creators can provide exclusive material that fans can access via memberships or one-time purchases.

This might contain bloopers, sponsor thank-yous, extended movies, dancing instruction, or studio tours. Platforms such as TikTok LIVE and Patreon, help distribute and monetise this extra material, giving producers a consistent revenue.

Creators can also get funding directly from fans through crowdfunding services or TikTok LIVE. Viewers can support them with tips, gifts, or by sponsoring projects. For example, a musician might use TikTok LIVE to raise funds for a new album, with fans donating to support the project and promote community togetherness.

Like wise, organizing live events, like workshops or collaborations with other creators, is another way to make money by selling tickets or getting sponsorships. These events could be video calls, presentations, or shows, allowing brands to create global events and monetize interactions through TikTok live streams. For example, a cooking influencer might host a live cooking class, selling tickets and partnering with kitchenware brands for sponsorships.

It can only get better as income can still be made by licensing content for ads, movies, or other media formats. This involves deals with production companies, brands, or media houses that want to use TikTok content for their ventures. For instance, a comedy creator might license their popular skits to a brand for use in a commercial, expanding their audience and revenue streams.

Professionals who have been using this application can provide consulting or a coaching session to learn how one can improve his or her account or handle a brand's account on TikTok. Services can be information planning or achieving, ways to interact with the audience, analysis of the collected data, or tips on working with the brand using their knowledge to help.

These monetization strategies indicate that when combined, it is possible to create multiple Income streams, this will dictate that the creators will not be depending on, for example, the TikTok income alone and therefore, leverage their TikTok to build a financially viable business.

In order to maximize income and remain relevant to the audiences while serving the brand partners at the same time, the key aspects have to be named: the constant search for new opportunities and the ability to follow the tendencies of the targeted audience, as well as being genuine.

CHAPTER 6

Case Studies of TikTok Success

This chapter is like getting an inside look at TikTok's hidden treasures—not gold, but viral content and social media stardom. It looks deep into how some TikTok accounts skyrocket from zero to hero. We're talking millions of followers, endless likes, and a virtual paradise of connections.

We'll break down what makes the most successful TikTok profiles rule the app and even the entire internet. We'll explore how these TikTok stars attract their audience and create magical branding moments. It's like having a backstage pass to your favorite TikTok sensations—every like and share contributing to the secret formula of going viral. So, sit back, relax, and dive into the stories of those who became TikTok legends. Who knows? Their success might just guide you to TikTok fame!

6.1. Analyzing Successful TikTok Accounts

Let's make it easy and go with Charli D'Amelio, the current reigning princess of TikTok dances. What's her charm or secret sauce? Perhaps most of all, it is about authenticity, trying to be one self and not the person that people want you to be. Charli is fluent and naturally performs these moves aware of the millions of people observing her, that is, she effortlessly dances her way into millions of hearts.

Lesson learned: realness wins more hearts than any 'like' button ever could.

Charli became famous after posting a video of herself dancing to K Camp's "Lottery (Renegade)". Her amazing dances and sheer enthusiasm drew everyone's attention on TikTok. The video went viral, receiving millions of views and likes virtually overnight. That's when Charli became viral on TikTok, earning millions of followers and becoming one of the platform's top influencers.

Her popularity was not just due to her dance abilities. Charli has a strong connection with her followers. She's always interacting with fans on live streams, reacting to comments, and collaborating with other TikTok stars. This genuine connection has resulted in a devoted audience that adores everything she does.

The success may also be attributed to her adept use of social media and collaborations with businesses. She's collaborated with huge brands like Dunkin' Donuts and Morphe Cosmetics, utilising her popularity to market their products in a way that seems authentic to her audience. These collaborations not only increase her trustworthiness, but they also allow her to meet new people outside of TikTok. Charli's experience demonstrates that being genuine, talented, and truly engaging with your audience are the keys to becoming successful on TikTok.

In the next stop, there he comes, Zach King, the video editing guru. His technique is fantastic, and I did stare at the screen a few times, wondering whether Hogwarts had a TikTok channel. Zach's secret? Out-of-the-box thinking that engages all five senses, physically reaching out and striking you. If one can get a reaction like "How did he do that?" for every video, one is on the right track.

In one of Zach most famous videos, he reaches into a mirror for a Starbucks coffee and takes out a genuine cup from its counterpart. This unique use of visual effects demonstrates not just his technical abilities, but also his flair for narrative, which appeals to people of all ages. Beyond his individual films, Zach's success stems from his unwavering innovation and ambition to push the boundaries of short-form storytelling. He is devoted to creating fun, family-friendly videos, which have gained him millions of social media followers. Collaborations with businesses like LEGO.

Disney illustrate his ability to seamlessly integrate items into his storytelling prowess.
The TikTok star also, Bella Poarch and her skills in lip-syncing is worthy to speak about. Greenspan's famous phrase "M for the B" was again recalled.

It was everywhere! As seen from Bella's performances, she dances expressively, focuses on lip-sync and posts contents that are the dream of everyone. As people can't help sharing the content you create and pass it to their crew, your number of fans will also increase. Emulating this path can help you resonate with many audiences, who appreciate authenticity and viral-worthy content that connects with their social circles.

Now focusing on content that is more specific, Tabitha Brown. Basically, she enjoys vegan food and positive energy and seeks the same. Tabitha has a very calming voice and the recipes she prepares makes one feel like they are being hugged by a Rain Coat. Her secret sauce? Be loyal to your traffic niche and make people smile all across the country, if not the world. Also, do people not remember Doggface208, the skateboard cranberry juice man? The guy's carefree ride with Fleetwood Mac playing struck a chord worldwide. The takeaway?

Simple setups and good vibes can go a long way in making something viral.
Let's mention Loren Gray as a person who rejoices in consistency. People are always complaining she has been dropping content bombs for ages now.

Nevertheless, from her explicit music videos to vlogs and behind-the-scenes glimpses, she knows exactly what keeps her fans engaged. Pro tip: continue swimming and getting better like Loren finding your groove that you should maintain. And when it comes to the funny bone, surely, one cannot disregard Lil Nas X here because his TikToks are just memes.

Whether he is sharing his new song promotion or posting funnyclips, he always kills it with the funny part. Never underestimate the joy of making peoples laugh, because laughter is indeed a way to people's heart.

In short, successful TikTok accounts have cracked the code with authenticity, creativity, engaging communication, consistency, and a dash of humor. Studying their strategies, content, and branding techniques can be invaluable for marketers.

So dive into the social media stream and mine TikTok's potential gold! Grab your smartphone, unleash your creativity, and who knows? You could be the next TikTok sensation, setting trends and earning likes on your path to success!

6.2. Lessons Learned from Top Creators

I suppose sometimes you also have pondered as to what makes the TikTok celebrities gather such a following?

It's all about authenticity. Authenticity on camera is something everyone connects with better than pretending to be what others want to see. If it's dancing, magic in the edit, or lip syncing, who people really are rises to the surface and makes regular people everywhere feel like a part of something. Therefore, you must remain authentic—the secret to growing your base of fans.

Creativity is another secret weapon. For example, companies are better positioned to encourage people to think creatively and generate unique ideas. One can utilize distortion or pull-off Henkel effects to leave viewers wondering, "Wait, how was that done?" Out of the box thinking usually catches the attention and focus. As a result, lesson learned: don't be scared to twist and surprise your visitors with unexpected content.

Engagement is essential. It's more than simply distributing content; it's also about connecting with your fans. Engaging with comments, hosting live sessions, or collaborating with other content creators builds a community around your channel.

It also develops a bond, and consumers are always drawn to businesses that offer such features and benefits. Well, there is one thing you should know: TikTok is always a give-and-take environment.

Forget about everything else and just own the corner you are in. Catering to your niche, be it vegan dishes, uplifting messages, or funny jokes, standing out is what makes you remarkable. When posting content to the public domain, it is always advisable to ensure that the content being reposted on the website or social media page is relevant and offers value to the readers; this helps create trust and credibility within the niche.

Therefore, you need to understand what sets you apart from other creators and lean into it as this is your magic ticket to usefulness in TikTok.

Another core instrument which is challenging but at the same time rewarding is consistency. This is important because consistent sharing of content sustains audience attention and also you increased your followers.

Even with posting of videos or vlogs, or participating in new challenges, frequency is impressive and it build loyalty. It also acts as brand association that strengthens identification and continues to build anticipation in your followers. You know what? Just keep the momentum going!

Moreover, the foolishness of the matter must not be dismissed at the end. Humor has no language and cultures all over the world can unite by sharing and enjoying good jokes.

As a result of incorporating humor into the videos, they will be fun, have comments that cut through the hearts and good feelings to friends which will make the videos shareable. Yes, laughter really has the most profound and positive impact more often than not in the TikTok world.

CHAPTER 7

Growing User Base and Engagement on TikTok

Boost your TikTok following and utilising metrics for success is your important approach to increasing TikTok effect.

In this chapter, we'll look at how to cultivate a strong and loyal following using data analytics; Discover how knowing analytics such as likes, shares, and comments can help you improve your content strategy and increase brand awareness on TikTok.

Unravelling TikTok's algorithm and audience preferences will provide you with insights on how to improve your approach and increase engagement. Prepare to turn data into concrete tactics that will take your TikTok presence ahead.

Prepare to unveil another mysteries of TikTok success, one analysis at a time! So grab your data analysis tools and get set for a journey into the heart of TikTok's dynamic landscape, where every click and share holds the key to expanding your reach and influence.

7.1. Growing User Base and Engagement on TikTok

Okay then, do you wish to become the dream TikTok star? Well, well, well let me tell you because here we are going to explain how you can expand your circle and make those hearts pop like Corden's confetti!

So let's start with some basics and this will be the first part of the article on how to gain more members to your TikTok. The idea of leveraging posts is simply to get users to look at them and say, 'Wait, this is gold!'

If one thinks about the TikTok app, people are invited to the party, but it's also about making people not just come to the party but also to dance. So no matter if you're trying out new tricks with skater on your board or practicing to hit THAT move in a dance you enjoy, find your frequency.

Now, how do you ensure that people come back for the next episodes or subsequently view other productions or creations on the platform? It's all about participation, especially if you're beautiful or handsome.

It is not just the case of putting up posts and waiting for the results; It's about getting in touch with your fans.

Engage with them through the comments section on video, ask them some questions maybe even tell them something is coming next and keep them in suspense. Just imagine a game night kind of proposal – the further engaged and entertained you make them, the more they're going to enjoy staying with you.

Oh, and to finish the list, what would we do without hashtags, trends, the most relevant music and other wonderful things?

These, however, are similar to the secret of removing the curtain and becoming recognized. It is preferable to publish using hashtags that show your individuality and check for trends (check Chapter 4 for details). Jump on the bandwagon like a famished rat that has been introduced to the lovely smell of bread - quickly! And it is the greatest method to ensure that your newfound audience notices you and sees all you've been producing.

Regarding analytics, they are not exclusive to math aficionados or nerds but applies to whoever takes into account numbers when budgeting. What do a maid, plumber, and typing teacher have in common with TikTok trends? Well, they're your tickets to it in a way. Analytics show you people are engaging with your videos and give you precious information such as who is watching, when and why.

At the moment, it can be compared to carrying a crystal ball through which one can guess the next hit song. One has to understand that strategizing is not a one-time exercise and should constantly monitor which activities are effective and which ones are not, in terms of audience growth.

Now, let's talk strategy. Do you know what a buddy system is? It's not that it's only used for field trips alone. Team up with other like-minded individuals, or your creative synergy will be as off as bread and jam. It is mutually beneficial because you both share each other's audience and makes your fans intrigued, and who knows, you guys could create the next big meme.

And here is a pro tip: don't be frightened of being random. This means that it is feasible to apply several ways while building anything. The crucial message for comprehending TikTok, with all of its intricacy and variety, is as follows: Variety is the flavour of TikTok existence.

The influence of offering viewers with unexpected content on occasion. It keeps people on the tip of their seats, eager for more. Keep in mind that you are not only publishing videos; you are also creating a subscriber list that will be more possessive than a puppy with a bone.

Branding will ultimately focus on the 'last mile' – or longevity – of a product, that is the ability of the brand-item to endure. I may or may not have seen the 'Rome in a day' meme doing the rounds on TikTok and thus, a TikTok empire is not built in a day either.

If you want to achieve something big, it is important to be consistent, my friend. I do not think that there are any strict rules of advertising that you have to follow – just make sure to keep going, continue providing material, and continue considering it a sort of entertainment. The more effort and passion one admires in the exercise, the more delicious the results will be. Well then, get ready to embark on this exhilarating ride to becoming the next TikTok superstar.

7.2. Strategies for Organic Growth
First of all, there's the concept that is an essential part of the whole process which has been mentioned

several times, It is the matter of authenticity. You don't need to use it as a phrase; it is a distinctive factor for you.

Get down to the real you and try not to make a staged appearance of what people want to see. Simple is what users on TikTok want desperately like they need the cup of coffee in the morning – people need to feel genuine, real.

Take Sarah, a TikTok maker who rose to prominence by embracing sincerity. Instead of following trendy trends, she offered personal events from her daily life, such as culinary disasters or amusing canine antics, which connected with viewers looking for authentic material. Sarah's approach enabled her audience to relate to her on a personal level, resulting in more likes, shares, and follows.

By being true to herself, Sarah not only created a dedicated network, but also garnered business partnerships seeking to collaborate with genuine influencers. Her TikTok success story demonstrates how authenticity can drive organic development and foster meaningful relationships with a wide range of audiences.

Second, bring forth timing to the stage. Perhaps, you have been involved in posting a video at 3 AM without understanding why it wasn't viral? Timing matters, folks. Make sure that you are in sync with when your audience is most responsive; this is important. Perhaps it is in between meals when workers have some free time or right before bedtime when people have nothing better to do.

Always upload your content when your viewers are likely to be in need of it, then be sure to get those view figures going up.

Now, let's add spice to our test preparations; let's try to be creative now. It is worth emphasizing that TikTok is a platform where extremely creative ideas are possible, so do not hesitating to get carried away. Can I try out a different structure of the video, a different kind of story to tell, or even a different kind of post-production. Take your audience off guard and put them constantly on the back foot. As long as the process of studying remains unexciting, so far as inspiration and creativity are concerned, it is a thing of the past.

People interacting, people engaging – it is not just a one-way traffic. The post should be treated in a conversational manner like how you would engage a friend at a party.

Engage with others and start discussions, encourage conversations and create a friendly environment. Doing this makes your followers involved and would make them have a better feeling of being part of the growth of the company, this is organic growth that any business person would wish to happen.

It would be negligent of me not to mention the TikTok trends that have swept the internet. Clear and change as the four seasons of the year, and following the trends provides a fantastic opportunity for your visibility. For immediate ideas, look to popular trends and add your own twist to give it a unique touch.

The sensation you get when you finally disclose something you've been working on for a long time; some people dance to music, whereas I write for applause. Remember to identify what kind of videos are succeeding, know your audience, and adjust your marketing approach accordingly. It is not playing darts; it is strategic planning that should be the norm for any unique business solutions.

And that is the guide on how to grow TikTok account naturally; as natural as fresh air on a hot sunny morning. This means remain genuine, keep trying and experimenting and hey, the process of becoming a TikTok star of course is a fun one regardless! TikTok your kingdom, create the magic they are seeking, and go out into the world!

7.3. Utilizing Analytics for Growth

Okay TikTokers, let's get into the geeky side of things and look into the numbers and analytics so that you can continue to grow your Tiktok. First, always consider analytics as your partner in the wilderness of TikTok and the six steps as tools to assist you. Well, they are not mere digits; they are your guide to the behaviours, interests, preferences, and needs of your audience.

To navigate your analytics dashboard, use it as a clue trail to a detective role-play to find your way. Conclusion involves the validation of the video through assessing results such as watch time, completion rates, and the audience. It is not mere information that you gather and present, but it is you road-map to creating contents that speak for it.

There is, however, one thing that you should be particularly careful with, and that is the rate at which you're gaining followers. It's similar to monitoring the pulse of your TikTok experience, it really is! See the rate at which you are getting more followers and what type of content increases those numbers the most.

Understanding this helps you make better adjustments towards your content and have other folks flock to your page like bees to honey.

Do you get the meaning of the phrase that states that know your audience? Well, analytics allows you to do that. Explore the deeper audiences to know all about who is watching your video – their age, gender, location, interest and the likes. This isn't about picking rigid categories; it is about making content that directly resonates with your people. When their likes and dislikes are best fitted by the subject of the specific video, they watch in a more excited manner.

Moving to the last of the big three, let me discuss content performance. Data show us which of the videos users adore and which of the videos requires more attention.

Looking at the traffic source, find out the regularities in your best traffic-generating content. So is it the format that we are unusual with or is it the topic or is it something to do with the editing style?

Leverage these findings to do more of what works and better understanding the mechanisms by which change occurs.

Take Jake, for example, who discovered that his comedic sketches based on relevant everyday circumstances frequently generated strong interaction. Jake discovered commonalities in his most popular material by analysing his traffic sources and viewer interactions, whether it was the unique format, hot themes he addressed, or his editing style. Armed with this insight, Jake concentrated on developing additional content that incorporated these winning qualities, resulting in greater views and follower engagement.

This proactive strategy not only increased Jake's TikTok visibility, but also provided him with insights into forecasting the next viral smash.

Specifically, engagement metrics are always beneficial if you want to measure the audience's level of activity.

Monitor the engagement level of your posts such as likes, comments, and shares cast by your audience. Are they commenting that they are laughing or they are sharing this or that post and tagging friends? Especially be attentive for those cues to establish a social context and thus promote the continuous flow of conversation.

Now, the highlighted algorithm is TikTok's mystical power that chooses who appears on the For You page. Analysis provides probable hints of how the algorithm perceives the information. Pay attention to 'views per video' and 'average viewing time.' This manner, the longer the viewer remains, the more TikTok rewards you with visibility to the user's consumed material. Pay this code a visit and you'll be halfway to virality.

Finally, let's speak about benchmarks. You may also track your development by measuring your performance indicators throughout different time periods.

Set goals for the amount of followers, retweets, likes, and views of the posted videos. Analytics are about creating objectives and aiming for the greatest results, not just reflecting on the past. And there, ladies and gents, concludes the brief and thorough tutorial on using analytics to improve your TikTok performance.

Simply take in the data, use these strategies, and utilise it to build your own TikTok Empire. While the conversation is centred on numbers, it is also about understanding the target audience, improving content, and sparking a revolution in the TikTok galaxy. Now that you are armed with analytics insight, go and win the battle even if it is a business one.

7.4. Adjusting Your Strategy Based on Data

It is important to know that data doesn't mean some numbers that have no relation to your life, absolutely, it is the opposite, they are your guide in the great ocean of TikTok content.

When trying to find usable information in your analytics, make sure to compare given facts with other facts in a way that leads to the identification of successful and unsuccessful elements.

Perhaps your comedy sketches bring traffic, while DIY tutorials do not do the same for your TikTok account.

This should be used for altering your focus on what you create to match with what your page's followers are interested in.

Audience retention is another important yardstick that holds large potential when it comes to tracking consumer behavior metrics. If you see a steep decline early in the videos, there probably is an issue with your hook or the speed you engage on the videos. Try out various forms of intros or recounting interlinking stories so that the audience remains fascinated from the beginning till the end.

Imagine you're scrolling through TikTok and you come across a video that starts with a catchy beat and a quick, funny intro about a relatable school scenario. If the video immediately grabs your attention and keeps you watching, that's a good hook.

However, if the video starts with a slow, uninteresting intro, you might scroll away quickly. To keep your audience engaged, try starting your videos with a meme, a surprising fact, or a funny story that resonates with everyday life, like a humorous take on online classes or a trending challenge.

This way, you keep your audience hooked right from the start.

Another valuable inlay in the data treasure case is comments and shares, which include a feedback loop. Agree with Kacie's excellent advice for communicating with audiences; the last one is about watching the feelings your audience expresses. Are they enjoying your latest dancing challenge or are they wondering about behind-the-scenes information we haven't yet shared?

Accept feedback as an intelligent businessperson assessing all information gathered about clients. It lays the basis for how you want to develop and share content that will spark discussions and convert people into fanatics.

It is also important to note time. Information shows when your audience is likely to be online and should be targeted with your marketing messages. Use this intel to plan when to post on your TikTok account.

Ideally, try to do it during the hours when your audience is most active consuming the information whether it is during lunch breaks or during night time. Also, consider shifting trends. Sometimes, it is just a matter of finding the next trend, and here, TikTok moves as fast as fashion seasons, which means that if you fail to act according to them, your strategy might fail as well.

It is important that at any given point you be in touch with what is trending in the particular niche and try and incorporate it in your content. There is nothing wrong with going for trends but the aim should not be to go for them blindly but to look for ways of how to strategically 'surf' with them and will your ability to express your personality.
Audience demography is clearly revealed, thanks to analytics.

Find out who you are reaching out to-being aware of their age, location, and their interests.

This bit provides information on how best to construct content that can appeal to different niches in your target market. In the case of a Gen Z audience or even millennial receiving content from pre-millennium, adapt to their language and watch the click-through rate go high.

Finally, test out all the tips and tricks you have in mind. Data-driven decision making looks at challenges from the perspective of developing ideas and fine-tuning your actions in response to fresh discoveries. Practice with new writing styles, discuss various topics, and then track the movement of your readers. One of the most distinguishing characteristics of TikTok is that some methods that are effective today can change in the near future.

Be as adaptable as possible, constantly discovering something new from your data, and begin working towards TikTok's success.

So, use analytics to understand and improve your TikTok process. Keep up with what your followers enjoy so you don't become outdated. Through full utilization of data, you're not just gaining followers—you're building a long-lasting TikTok presence and brand (which will be discussed in the next chapter).

CHAPTER 8

Creating a Consistent Brand Image

Making your videos relatable completely transforms your TikTok image and ensures that every single video you submit is easily recognised as your own. If there is one chapter that summarises entire text, it is this one: all components of the platform must be consistent in order to establish a cohesive brand identity.

From the colour palette you want to utilise to the fonts, filters, and unique voices that characterise your brand, we will show you how to achieve consistency in both visual and narrative aesthetics.

However, this may be simply stated as giving your account a distinct, recognisable appearance that TikTok users can quickly identify! Brace yourself for some branding because it's time to buff your brand to a brilliant height.

8.1. Defining Your Brand Identity

Let me break down how you can make your brand POP like a disco stick on TikTok. And those sales pitches that go like this: 'Wow, whoa, I need more of that flash, that glitz, that bling-bling to stimulate my purchasing power.

First things first: *Brand identity* – what exactly is this? People like to think of it as simply the overall energy, or the general energy of certain items. That is how you want to be perceived, recognised, and defined by people when you enter a place or see your image on a media screen.

Consider a noisy event in a large hall filled with people, in such an event people still make an attempt to listen to the main speaker; your brand concept is the way to stand out as the main speaker and as a drop in the ocean.

Think of it as your own personal emoji combo: the colors, the typeface, the tone, and even the way you present things are all part of your brand's overall look.

For example, if your brand could be expressed in meme-form, how would it look? That's your identity, fam. If your TikTok content were a vibe, would it be the chill lo-fi study beats or the energetic dance challenges?

Imagine your brand as a series of emojis—each one representing a different aspect of your content. Maybe it's the fire emoji for your hottest takes, the laughing emoji for your comedy skits, or the sparkle emoji for your beauty tutorials. This unique blend is what sets your brand apart and makes it instantly recognizable to your audience.

To define your TikTok brand, ask yourself these questions: What makes my content unique? What kind of vibe do I want my audience to resonate with? Are you here to spread comedy and knowledge, or just to be fly and cool?

Your answers will shape your brand. For instance, if you're quick with witty responses and trending challenges, that will reflect in the energy of your TikTok presence. Knowing your brand identity helps you create content that truly connects with your audience.

Now, let us discuss aesthetics. Oh, you are correct; we are moving to the look department, if you wish.

Choose your colours carefully; they are just as significant as the clothes a brand wears. Do you prefer colourful lights and endless pleasure, or a monochromatic, cool, and elegant environment? Consider how friendly or creative you want to come across while selecting a font.

Tightly wrapped and sophisticated or tight and rebellious? That is the question. All of these elements contribute to the environment you want others to expect or pick up from you.
But wait, there's more! Consistency is key. Just like a catchy song hook, keeping your style, colors, and fonts the same across your TikTok builds trust and makes your brand memorable.

This consistency helps you stand out in the crowded digital space and in TikTok space in particular. So, make sure your vibe stays the same throughout your content to keep your audience coming back for more.

Don't forget your voice. No, not the one you or I would sing in the shower.

Your brand voice is the way or manner colloquially used by a brand to communicate with the public. Do you rock weirdness, or fun? Chill and laid-back? Or maybe it just might be you, the hype beast getting everybody amped up. Whatever it is, own it like it's your own banga. Whatever it is, own it like it is something special that is associated with you.

In addition, keep growing. The digital world moves even faster than trends on television platforms such as TikTok. Overemphasis on such topics should be done with consideration for what your audience enjoys.

The idea is that brands should adapt, flexible and not be rigid, even if the shift is a normal part of the development cycle. Just remember that every meme, no matter how huge or popular, is only excellent if it remains topical, hip, and amusing.

Well, that's all I have to say. Your brand is your energy, and so throw the shades like the confetti of New Year.

8.2. Visual Consistency and Themes

Now, let me take you to the most entertaining and creative part of making your brand sparkle like a diamond — visual Brand Consistency and Brand Themes.

This is where your TikTok grid becomes as visually appealing as a beautifully fine art. Such consistency is like having one's own style of seeing things and approaches to their representation.

It is what makes them coherent visually, so you would know at first glance that they are all part of the same marketing campaign. In this case, it can be described as the bond that connects everything that happens within your TikTok reality.

Let me give you a real-life example. I followed a TikToker who always used a vibrant color scheme and quirky fonts. Every time I scrolled through their grid, it felt like walking into a neon-lit arcade.

Their consistency made it super easy to recognize their videos at a glance. One day, they posted a video without their usual style, and it felt out of place, like seeing a zebra at a penguin party!

Keeping your visual themes consistent not only makes your content look professional but also helps in building a loyal audience who can spot your videos instantly, no matter where they are in the feed.

Next is the theme. By thinking of themes, TikTok becomes like having the record of songs that a DJ has to play in your channel.

They provide your content with a certain style, and focus on the overall look of your work. Perhaps you prefer practical tips on how to change a light bulb, or an everyday video blog, or just simple jokes—whatever you decide, it is your niche.

For more instances, imagine you're passionate about DIY projects. Your theme could revolve around creative home hacks and step-by-step tutorials on making everything from homemade decor to fixing a leaky faucet.

This focused approach not only establishes you as an expert in your niche but also attracts followers who are eager to learn and engage with your practical tips.

In a similar manner create a variety of contents but design it in a consistent way with the brand. Try a landscape from a different perspective, or different lenses, or post processing technique. Though no one is entirely sure of what to expect they should always be intrigued by that familiar taste they expect from you. For example, if your TikTok channel focuses on travel and adventure, you could showcase destinations from unconventional angles, such as aerial drone shots or time-lapse videos. Despite the variety in your content, your audience should always recognize your signature style—a blend of stunning visuals, insightful commentary, and maybe a touch of humor.

And you may want to also include your logo or any watermark that you have. I found it like your personal mark—the one you get inked on your skin but, this is virtually engraved on your presence online.

You should use it in your videos, preferably in a conspicuous position to reaffirm your brands' image on your videos. It is your corner in the TikTok universe.

Moreover, another related issue is that of thumbnails. Think of them as the movie posters for your TikTok videos. Thumbnails are the small images that viewers see before they click to watch your video. Just like movie posters, they need to grab attention quickly. Use bright colors and bold, easy-to-read text. As you may know, cooking up some catchy, pop tunes is essential to our mission. Choose bright, readable colors for text and make the fonts as flashy as possible with pictures that shout out,

"Hey, you, click on me, I look cool!"

If your TikTok video is about a delicious recipe, your thumbnail could feature a mouth-watering close-up of the finished dish with the recipe title in large, vibrant letters.

This visual appeal encourages viewers to click and watch your content. Pro tip: It can easily be managed by using templates or presets every time to make sure that there is a steady flow without confusion. For editing the images you can use apps like Canva or Adobe Spark to make your images look more professional.

They enhance the ease with which you create thumbnails and also edit the videos you produce, saving you time to do what you do best; producing quality content.

It is necessary for you to read something about filters and effects before proceeding with your treatment of them. They undoubtedly add flavour to your TikTok videos. Consider them more as extras that can help to liven up your videos without completely altering the overall tone of your brand's channel.

Whether it's a cinematographic aesthetic or a surrealist look, make sure it suits the overall style of the work. In essence, let me repeat myself: Making your images consistent is not just about styling but establishing trust with the viewers.

When the audience starts to watch your videos, they should be able to immediately tell who you are as if they are quickly identifying their friend in a crowded place.

Themes and visual compatibility together act as your safety mechanism to success in the world of online traffic. Unless this changes, remain loyal to your visuals, think of themes that you can explore and sprinkle your fairy dust on all your videos.

8.3. Authenticity, Voice and Building Trust with Your Audience

Authenticity has been emphasised sufficiently to demonstrate that it is worthwhile. it is not just a buzzword; it's the key to making your mark on TikTok. The first step in defining authenticity is to identify your place in the game - who you are and what rules you have decided to follow.

Do you want to be the silly or naughty character, the intelligent one, or just the ordinary superhero you see around you? You should be natural not just in terms of how you dress and talk, but also in terms of humoring and enjoying your personality as much as any audience would. In case you do not know this, audiences can tell when you're genuine.

Also, your voice is what you use to communicate directly with others or to engage in discussions. Do you believe it's just fancy jokes and memes? Are you ever at a loss for words and speak as if you've returned as Confucius, the eastern master? Or maybe you're the cheerleader, inspiring everyone like it's an Alabama football game, you know, the crazy enthusiastic crowd.

Command your voice as if it were yours alone, just like your favourite trainers are.

Consider how Sarah uses her voice on TikTok to engage her audience authentically. She shifts effortlessly between humorous anecdotes that aligns like well-timed memes and moments of wisdom akin to Confucius, offering profound insights.

At times, she adopts the role of a spirited cheerleader, rallying her followers with the enthusiasm of an Alabama football game. Sarah's ability to command her voice across these different tones and styles allows her to connect deeply with her audience, much like beloved mentors who inspire and guide through their distinct voices and perspectives.

Whether you're sharing stories, reacting to trends, or discussing topics you're passionate about, authenticity shines through when you're genuinely engaged. It's not just about entertaining; it's about creating a space where others feel welcome and valued. So, be true to yourself, embrace your voice, and watch as your authenticity draws others in on TikTok and beyond.

Let's speak about trust, which is the cement that holds your audience together, or, to put it another way, the superglue on a shattered piece of furniture. To acquire people's trust, you must understand that it is not about putting on your finest performance; it is about demonstrating to be trustworthy, genuine, and consistent in every video you submit.

First, it outlines the measures that representatives must follow: First, keep your promises. If you inform your audience that you'll be publishing a new dance instructional every Friday, they'll expect to see you groove to the rhythm every Friday.

I believe that consistent and predictable methods generate trust in the same way that chocolate chip cookies build smiles; it is unavoidable.

Be as transparent as a glass of water; there should be no barrier or cloud between you and your audience. Mention how you came up with the concept, the process behind your creation, and scream out if you made a mistake. Yes, scream. The audience is more open to errors than when a work or a person is overly polished. Let's consider Alex, a TikTok creator known for his DIY crafting videos.

He embodies transparency by openly sharing his creative process from concept to completion. In his videos, Alex explains how he brainstormed the idea, the materials he used, and even showcases any mistakes he made along the way—sometimes with a comical scream. This approach not only humanizes his content but also fosters a genuine connection with viewers who value honesty and relatability in social media personalities.

To build trust, reply to comments, call out some of your followers, or even thank them. Audience develops trust, so make sure they reply and share the same sentiment, that they respect what you're doing. Authenticity strikes again!

Forget the illusion of popularity and pretending to be someone you are not only to obtain 'likes' and 'follows'. Artwork should reflect the artist's personal values, beliefs, and personality.

Another thing that the audience will never tolerate is you imitating a specific personality or anything that is not you; instead, always be yourself.

However, if your specialisation is mirroring or duplicating another personality, there is nothing fundamentally wrong with it.

In truth, authenticity in this case might refer to authentically reflecting the features of another persona or style. Just as actors bring fictitious characters to life, social media personas may accurately depict and celebrate the characteristics of respected personalities or styles.

The goal is to execute it effectively, conveying the essence and subtleties that aligns with your audience. This method can be used as an artistic homage or to investigate various aspects of creativity.

Also, whether you're channelling the spirit of a historical figure, a fictitious character, or a current icon, what counts most is your ability to connect with your audience and produce information that is interesting and informative and true to the persona you're embodying.

Let this always be in your mind when you create your content, quality over quantity. One amazing video is far more preferable than ten decent ones. Spend time and money in generating content, which is interesting and enjoyable for the readers, and depicts the mood of the brand. The trust is built over time and with the quality content being provided as well.

Collaborate like a pro. It is alright for you to collaborate with people whose works are similar to what you stand for and what you propagate. It is a proven fact that collaborations spread the word about your brand while new perspectives help you maintain and establish the trusted source of information status.

Moreover, showcase social proof. Share testimonials, reviews, or shoutouts from satisfied followers. Social proof builds trust by showing that others believe in your brand, making newcomers more likely to jump on board.

Be reliable as your Favorite delivery app. Stick to your posting schedule, deliver on your promises, and show consistency in your brand's message. Reliability builds trust over time, like building blocks stacking up to a sturdy tower.

Take Emma, a beauty influencer on TikTok, who effectively showcases social proof to build trust with her audience. Emma's followers see this positive feedback and feel more confident in trying out her suggestions. She is as reliable as a favorite delivery app—sticking to her posting schedule, delivering on her promises, and consistently maintaining her brand's message.

Over time, this reliability has built a strong foundation of trust, attracting more followers who know they can count on her for honest and valuable content.

In synopsis, I will advise you take this general tips, stay humble and stay hungry. No one likes a know-it-all. Stay open to feedback, learn from your mistakes, and keep evolving. Trust grows when your audience sees your genuine effort to improve and innovate. If you take a close look at Lily, a fitness coach on TikTok, who embodies the mantra "stay humble and stay hungry."

Despite her expertise, she always stays open to feedback from her followers, learns from her mistakes, and continuously evolves her content. Whether it's trying new workout routines or improving her video quality, Lily's audience sees her genuine effort to improve and innovate. This humility and drive to be better endear her to her followers, building trust and loyalty as they watch her journey of constant growth and authenticity.

Building trust with your TikTok audience is a marathon, not a sprint. Be authentic, deliver quality content, engage with your followers, and stay true to your values. Trust is the foundation that supports your brand's growth and longevity in the wild world of TikTok.

It is of vital essence to understand that trust with your TikTok audience is not a one-time effort but a journey that is long and winding. Be real, give your audience the best substance and interactivity, and remain genuine to purpose.

Trust remain the key on which your brand capitalizes in your journey to a sustainable existence in the somewhat wild, wild world of TikTok. So, go ahead, build those bonds, and watch your tribe grow stronger with every video you create.

8.4. Maintaining Brand Consistency and Evolution on TikTok

Maintaining a consistent brand image is critical for creating a devoted audience on TikTok, because the landscape is always shifting. Consistency implies that your audience understands what to anticipate from you, whether it's the tone of your videos, the style of your images, or the time of your updates.

While consistency is important, it's equally crucial to allow your brand to evolve. TikTok trends change rapidly, and what was popular a few months ago might not apply today.

So, balancing consistency with evolution is about understanding your brand's core values and being flexible with everything else. For instance, if your brand promotes positivity, explore different ways to convey this message through new challenges or trending formats.

This way, you're keeping your content fresh and engaging while staying true to what your audience loves about your brand.

In addition to consistency and evolution, several key practices can enhance your brand on TikTok. One of which is storytelling. Storytelling is a powerful tool; use it to share relatable experiences and success stories that align emotionally. Collaborations can also boost your brand by introducing it to new demographics and adding novelty. Stay true to your values, whether supporting causes, encouraging people, or simply making them laugh.

In short, I will summarize with this. Maintaining a consistent brand image on TikTok is key to building a loyal following. When your audience recognizes your visuals, tone, and posting schedule, it builds trust and familiarity.

Engage thoughtfully and regularly, but don't be afraid to evolve with trends to stay relevant. Balance consistency with adaptability by understanding your core values while experimenting with new content.

Be authentic, collaborate, and continuously improve. Ultimately, your brand's success on TikTok relies on being real, consistent, and flexible, creating content that resonates with your audience.

CHAPTER 9

Global Reach and Diversity on TikTok

TikTok isn't just an app, it's like a superpower for marketers hungry to reach a global audience. Picture it as this epic melting pot where K-pop fanatics, DIY maestros, cooking enthusiasts, and hilarious comedians all gather to create and share their magic. With over a billion active users, TikTok is like this crazy digital stage where cultures collide, creativity thrives, and every scroll leads to a new adventure.

It's where a dance from Seoul can inspire someone in São Paulo, a cooking hack from Tokyo can blow up in New York, and laughter crosses all borders. Get ready for TikTok: where every video has the power to captivate millions and where the next big thing is just a swipe away

.9.1 Understanding TikTok's Global Reach

TikTok's user base spans across numerous countries and regions, each with unique cultural worldviews and preferences. It will interest you to know that TikTok's global appeal is evident in its popularity across various regions such as North America, Europe, Southeast Asia, Africa and Latin America. Each of these regions showcases distinct trends, user behaviors, and content preferences.

Imagine, you're scrolling through your feed, grooving to a catchy beat from Brazil, learning a new dance move from Korea, and laughing at a meme that started in the USA but has now taken over the world. That's TikTok for you, a virtual passport to cultural exchange and trendsetting.

To create content that resonates deeply with local audiences, cultural sensitivity is key.

It's like being a respectful global guest. Imagine not showing up to a Japanese tea ceremony in a sombrero and cowboy boots, expecting everyone to join in the cha-cha slide! Cultural sensitivity involves a thorough grasp of local customs, languages, humor, and values.

What's hilarious in one culture might be offensive in another. To craft truly culturally relevant content, immerse yourself in local space, whether it's mastering dance moves or choosing the right attire. Embracing these differences not only builds trust and relevance with diverse audiences but also fosters a more inclusive and engaging TikTok community.

Consider Coca-Cola. Thus, Coca-Cola's #ShareACoke campaign became an international hit as a result of references to local traditions.

To make their argument, they inscribed the names of specific places on the bottles, as well as terms associated with those areas, such as Sydney or Shanghai. Coca-Cola urged social media users from all around the world to record themselves with personalized bottles using the specific hashtag.

So, if you want to go viral, you need to get local - or risk being the only one doing the cha-cha slide in a sea of salsa dancers! Remember that trends on TikTok are highly dynamic and can vary significantly from one region to another.

A dance trend popular in Europe might not catch on in Latin America, where a different style of content might be trending. You need to stay updated with local trends and adapt their content strategies accordingly.

Imagine scrolling through TikTok and stumbling upon a hilarious meme in Spanish. Even if you don't speak the language, the universal language of laughter connects us all. TikTok has this magical ability to translate jokes, trends, and heartfelt messages into a language everyone understands- 'emotions. Nevertheless, language and the right message can be the source of much success: that is a lesson that Samsung has learned well.

It is important to mention that their campaigns are international thus they use subtitles, multiple versions, and culturally specific images. It matters whether they are introducing a new smartphone model or presenting new technologies – Samsung's content multimedia is available and reveals the company's position from one country to another.

In a similar sense, Language can be a big barrier when reaching global audiences, but TikTok has some handy tools to help. Subtitles, translations, and universal visual storytelling can make your content accessible to more people. Use these tools to ensure everyone can understand and enjoy your content, no matter what language they speak, just like Samsung. Plus, it shows you care about inclusivity and accessibility.

So, whether you're fluent in multiple languages or just starting your journey with a few words of Spanish or French, TikTok celebrates your linguistic adventures.

It's a platform where communication isn't limited by borders—it's amplified by diversity. Grab your phone, practice your accent (or accents), and let's continue spreading laughter, knowledge, and love in every language imaginable on TikTok!

Think about it: you can start your morning with a motivational speech in Mandarin, take a midday break with a comedy skit in Portuguese, and end your day with a heartfelt message in sign language.

TikTok bridges gaps, breaks down barriers and reminds us that no matter where we're from, our voices deserve to be heard.

Moreover, different regions like different types of content, such as short skits, educational videos, or live streams. Knowing these preferences helps marketers design content that fits their audience's habits. For instance, North American viewers might like quick, snappy videos, while Southeast Asian users might prefer detailed, informative ones. Matching content to regional tastes can boost engagement and make marketing campaigns on TikTok more effective.

9.2. Strategies for Targeting Different Regions

Partnering with local influencers is a smart move. They know their audience's likes and can create relatable content. Influencers get the local trends, humor, and culture, making their posts more engaging.

Working with them helps brands gain trust and credibility in new markets and offers insights into local behavior and preferences.

For instance, a beauty brand entering Japan might team up with popular Japanese beauty influencers to promote products in line with local trends. Similarly, Nike has proved to be more efficient in the creation and implementation of regional communication strategies that speak directly to the consumer, coupled with a solid brand essence that cuts across the world.

In practice, their campaigns mainly focus on the local sportsmen and their success stories in Brazil they use soccer stars and in Japan, they use marathon runners.

Adidas makes use of local influencers to extend its global campaigns. With the help of local influencer cooperation, Adidas targets those regions and attracts customers who are tuned to the local tendencies.

Not only do they market the shoes but they act and speak exactly as the shoes company would want them to, which is in line with the social norms of the region.

Still speaking of the way of life – culture. Attempt to also use local symbols, slang, and references that sit well with the audience. For instance, an ad campaign in Mexico might incorporate traditional music or imagery that is widely recognized and appreciated locally. Also, maintaining a flexible approach that allows for quick adaptation to changing trends and feedback is essential.

TikTok moves fast, so what is popular today might be old news tomorrow. Brands need to stay flexible and adjust their strategies based on real-time feedback and new trends. This could mean tweaking content formats, trying out new styles, or even rethinking their target audiences as things change.

Cultural sensitivity is essential when creating content for various audiences. To begin, it would be prudent to conduct some basic research to ensure that your content is proverbial. Dive deeply into cultural operations in the targeted regions, as well as the client's unique characteristics and preferences.

Engage your colleagues, read through cultural analysis, and undertake extensive market research. Consider it the master document for your content development plan. Knowing your target is quite helpful in tailoring information that will be of interest to them.

Assume you're a worldwide food business looking to expand into the Middle Eastern market via TikTok. Before developing material, you perform extensive study on cultural norms, nutritional preferences, and culinary traditions in several countries within the region.

You interact with local food bloggers and chefs, read cultural assessments of dining customs and regional cuisines, and gain insights from market research on consumer behavior. With this information, you can adapt your TikTok content strategy to showcase Middle Eastern recipes, culinary techniques, and ingredients that are relevant to local tastes and preferences.

To point out what has been said further, genuineness is your ticket to the prize when it comes to TikTok marketing. Do not use stereotypes – they are unconstructive and can even cause harm. In fact, do not develop articles that you think will suit the black audience's specific ethnic or cultural background because this is a mistake.

Think of it like this: In other words, if you wouldn't like a person to stereotype your people, vice versa never help to stereotype other people. Stay honest, and viewers will know you are doing your best. To top it off, while it is good to make sure there is no contradiction in the brand message around the world, a little adjustment can contribute immensely. Include a message or image localization respectively to fit the reception of the campaigns in different countries.

In addition to the general understanding of languages, there is something known as global humor. Everyone can tell a joke, however the humor that is seen as hilarious varies even between neighboring countries. The sense of humor between New York and Tokyo differs significantly.

Thus, it is preferable to tailor your joke-telling to the environment of the place you are visiting. Consider employing jokes based on current memes, lingo, or anything else that the target audience will understand. Timing and recognizing regional differences in your issue can make your content roll on the floor with laughter. Also, try to create content in multiple languages as stated earlier. Subtitles and captions make content accessible to non-native speakers, so, consider that.

9.3. Leveraging TikTok's Features for Global Campaigns

The following are some of the features that TikTok has that can enable brands to effectively moderate and steer their campaigns all over the world. We can begin this way, TikTok Advert Manager is your ticket to the world of focused marketing.

It allows the brands to develop the exact form of advertisements with functions of location preferences. You can set goals about single areas of the world ranging from North America and Europe to other continents, plus, with the help of demographic targeting, choose just the required group of users. This is like giving your ads a map; you guide them where they are to go, and they will get to their destination-targeted customers in today's world.

The second key element is hashtag challenges. Hashtag challenges are social media initiatives that serve as social celebrations and can be tailored to specific geographical areas. Consider a dance challenge that becomes famous in New York, and then create a comparable version with a twist in Tokyo or London. Regional versions of global challenges should make use of local inventiveness and an awareness of current trends. In a way, it's as if you've organized a global disco event, and each city has developed its style of dancing.

Are trendsetters next on the list? This was a pretty fascinating point: TikTok can turn anyone into a celebrity overnight.

This is a quotation from Tim Ferriss: One minute you're posting a hilarious cat video, and the next your dance move is trending from New York to Nairobi.

Yes, they have superpowers such as the ability to fly or immense strength, but instead, Laroy makes people laugh and doubles meaning by dancing to the beat of the new vibe. In addition to this, TikTok analytics gives you what you need to know about your content at the backend as it operates across the world.

Submerge yourself in engagement rates, viewers, and the trends that exist in various regions to allow for adjustments. It is as if you were holding a crystal ball that shows you where and how you are favorable – allowing you to tailor your strategy and increase your effect across all markets.

Furthermore, unique effects and filters can add localized components to global advertising efforts. Consider creating a filter that resembles Japanese art or a sticker that represents Mexico. Not only can these features boost the level of participation in your material, but they also offer your viewers the impression that they are reading content tailored to their specific region.

In some ways, it's similar to providing your audience with an engaging way to interact with your brand and own it. For example, viral dance, memes, and music. It's also as if your brand becomes the newest and most desirable kid on the social 'block' or joins the 'coolest club' that everyone in town is talking about till the latest trend moves on to the next city.

As a result, by optimizing these elements, marketers can create effective global TikTok campaigns that appeal to a variety of audiences and increase brand popularity internationally.

9.4. Inclusive Representation

Yes, TikTok is about trends, but it is also about representation, inclusivity, and the incredible diversity of humanity. They cannot afford to treat representation based on race, gender, sexual orientation, religion, or any other minority as an afterthought. TikTok gets it.

When it comes to body positivity, identity, social causes like LGBTQ+ issues or mental health, or publishing tales from people of color, the platform is a place where everyone has a voice.

The fact is that what is more impressive is how people are given a chance to take back stories and rewrite aesthetics with TikTok. TikTok is a celebration of culture, wherein people are free to share their stories such as retaining the cultural dance that passed down from their young age and sharing transformation ideas.

Think of a Grandmother showing her grandchild how to do native dance moves or a story about a person embracing themselves. That is why TikTok is a platform that turns everyday life into magic.

This takes me to the creators, on whose shoulders the wonderful notion of the publisher rests. TikTok is a platform for pioneers who are changing the way their communities are represented. They are more than just influencers; they are messengers, ambassadors, and philosophers who spread the message, fight for others, and refuse to allow people to be locked in the cage of someone else's opinion.

Consider an artist who uses comedy to combat prejudice about mental health issues, or an artist who uses exquisite henna designs to demonstrate the richness of his or her culture. These creators represent the heart and soul of TikTok.

Therefore, the inclusivity that TikTok enthusiasts promote doesn't merely boil down to the trending word. Since it is about accepting diversity, fighting against injustice, and valuing individuality and people's contributions.

TikTok is where they don't just embrace you for who you are, but appreciate you and patronize you. So, no matter whether you are teaching others the recipes of your ancestral cuisine, raising awareness of social justice issues through poetry, or even making people happy with your laughter, TikTok is your stage. It is a place for people of all backgrounds to call home and for which every video has the potential to inspire the change we want to see in this world we live in.

It's not just a fun activity – reaching across the globe can be a key advantage for brands and content makers. Its use of influencers in different areas and trending subjects that can be of interest to people around the globe makes TikTok an endless opportunity to disseminate your information to the targeted individuals. Think about using an innovative idea and initiating a simple step dance challenge that goes transcontinental or participates as a collaborator with other global designers from different parts of the world. That is why the stage of TikTok will help your message to stand out and be truly influential.

Moreover, Small companies that want to expand internationally will find value in TikTok's collaborations, as will artists in search of inspiration and new markets. For example, a cafe in Seattle working with a Japanese barista influencer to come up with a cross-cultural coffee appreciation or a physical artist in Paris collaborating with a Brazilian digital artist to blend past and contemporary art. This is the place where innovation does not sleep, and every collaboration can become viral among millions of people.

Thus, pack your passport if you are serious (or your phone), search for a partner at the other end of the earth, and let us do something incredible on TikTok.

Let's imagine a fashion designer in Milan collaborating with a streetwear specialist in Seoul to bring the latest fashionable tops to the market, or a comedian in New York partnering with a mime artist in Paris to make a funny, international video skit.

Altogether you must prove to this world that creativity has no location and the most unique ideas appear when the cultural differences unite in the most lovely way. Let's keep moving forward, creating, learning, and sharing ideas no matter within continents, language barriers, and/or geographic separations. Whether you're in the kitchen boiling water for the chef from Bangkok, or creating music with a DJ from Berlin, TikTok is your platform.

CHAPTER 10

Educational Resources and Algorithm Tips

As TikTok continues to dominate the social media sphere, the demand for comprehensive guides and educational resources on TikTok marketing has surged. Imagine stepping into the wild, vibrant world of TikTok, where every swipe reveals a new trend and every like is a stepping stone to fame. Don't worry, we're not just sending you in unarmed.

We've got a lot of guides, courses, and webinars to help you navigate this digital jungle. Think of this chapter as your personal tour guide, decoding the mystical "For You" page and unveiling the secrets of the TikTok algorithm. So, grab your phone and let's crack the code together—your next video could be the one that makes you famous!

10.1. How the TikTok Algorithm Works

To most users, and particularly those seeking to popularize their brands, understanding how the TikTok algorithm works can be compared to the recipe for success. So, it is not a coincidence, it is a system set in motion to keep users engaged in their "For You" section. VIDEOS 'suited' to the user's preference and behavior; TikTok feeds the users video suggestions that can make it feel like the latter is practically known by the app.

Here is the scoop: It's worth noting again that the TikTok algorithm flourishes when you interact with the content. It changes itself based on the stuff you like, share, and watch to give you a feed of comparable content.

The more interactions you have, such as liking, commenting, and sharing, the more TikTok provides you with content you enjoy. I know it is, so don't be bashful and give those videos some views. Similar to watch time, watched time is TikTok's primary measure.

The more time you spend watching a video, the more likely it is to be pushed by the algorithm. This is why it is critical to grab the best audience as soon as possible and keep them engaged for the duration of the commercial.

But wait, there's more: it takes into account features of the TikTok post, such as the caption, hashtags, and effects, before uploading the video to the TikTok recommendation system. Just make sure that your content is something your audience would like to watch and concentrate on issues that are ' trendy' — they like that you know.

If you're not familiar with this concept, let me tell you that consistency is a friend. You must post frequently and show TikTok that you enjoy making your viewers laugh. Maintain a routine that works for you, but remember: there is a phrase that says it is better to have few good things than to have many less good things any day. Make each post count!

Furthermore, trends and problems cannot be overlooked, especially when doing a SWOT analysis of an organization. Following the latest trend can quickly increase your view count; it's as if we're all in on the biggest inside joke, don't you think, TikTokers?

Collaborations also attract algorithmic attention. Collaborate with others, create a duet based on a viral song, or solve a problem together. This is more than just expanding your audience; it is about developing a demographic that TikTok cannot refuse to promote.

Remember, TikTok is all about short, snappy content. You've got a tiny window to grab someone's attention, so make it count. Start with a bang—something that makes people stop scrolling and say, "Wait, what?"

Whether it's a catchy hook, a surprising fact, or an unexpected twist, you need that initial spark to pull viewers in. Once you've got their attention, keep the energy high. Think of it like a rollercoaster ride; there should be no dull moments.

That's it for the TikTok algorithm. Memorize these tips and continue to test them, and 'bingo!' your TikTok content will soar. Who knew that making one's favorite activity into the world's golden sensation could be so entertaining? We'll break it down and make waves with the most enjoyable application in the history of apps!

10.2. The Growing Demand for Educational Resources

You should be more aware by now, as TikTok is not just the app that your young niece or nephew uses to perform hilarious motions. It is the real deal, and it is a powerful platform for marketers and businesses. But here's the catch: as we all know, mastering TikTok, like many other social networks, isn't as simple as posting a humorous new video of a cat and expecting a lot of likes.

Unfortunately, it is an entirely other universe that necessitates a completely different strategy. Sorry for the lull in rhythm, but this is when the need for educational resources comes into play.

Consider this: marketing and corporate groups are feverishly acting like contestants vying for the secret formula of this well-known social media platform. They want to discover what makes it unique, the unseen formulas, and, most importantly, the techniques for capturing a viewer's attention in a matter of seconds.

As a result, consumers saw a significant increase in the number of ebooks, online manuals, and other resources geared at promoting businesses via TikTok. What if I told you that these materials are TikTok reality hacks that will teach you how to create posts that not only capture people's attention but also make them remember?

Online classes and webinars? Oh, they're the most valuable players here. Consider these TikTok boot camps, where you enroll and are guided through the specifics by experienced trainers. It's like having a 'personal assistant' who understands your needs, but instead of getting you in shape, they improve your TikTok performance.

The final category comprises blogs and articles—they are your gossipy friends. They lay out everything you need to know about TikTok's most popular trends and newer skills.

Podcasts and video series? Terms like 'learning,' 'teaching,' and 'education' that could have been relics of traditional teaching and learning processes are likewise replaced with badges as if they were backstage credentials to TikTok education. They show you behind-the-scenes activity, including genuine illustrations and interviews with pros.

Yes, hearing these wonderful creators and learning from them is like listening in on their secrets while they create. As for me, TikTok marketing communities on social media are out of the question. These are your new squad, your new crew, where you may share tales, and suggestions on how to deal with various challenges and devise new tactics. And it's like having a network of friends who are all striving to understand TikTok alongside you.

Research and case studies? These are detective novels in the marketing world. They take the time to explain why some TikTok ads are successful while others are not, as well as why these differences exist.

They can be defined as a map that stops you from making mistakes and demonstrates other people's successful techniques. Is there a certification or credentials for TikTok marketing? Those I said are your badges of honor.

They demonstrate to the world that you have what it takes to create pieces that can sway the general audience. It's as if one earns his or her stripes and is granted access to the TikTok community.

What about interactive workshops and hackathons? This is where all of a company's operations take place. They're similar to other group activities in that you get to get your hands dirty while working with fellow TikTok enthusiasts.

It is engaging, and artistic, and frequently results in the creation of the' meme of the century.' When it comes to TikTok promotion, worldwide events and forums might be regarded as championships.

These are the gatherings where the top thinkers and doers gather to compare notes, demonstrate, brag, and forecast. It's networking gold, people. The connections below can help your TikTok choreography become global.

In other words, the requirement for TikTok marketing education demonstrates the extent to which it influences brand presentation modification.

You can get the most out of TikTok and its tricks by using the resources available in manuals, classes, examples, and community assistance. It is the distinction between superficial popularity, which temporarily captivated the fans' likes and creating their wave on the world wide web.

As a result, whether you're in your first week or year, there's a lot to learn if you want to improve your skills. Take the plunge and immerse yourself in the research to better understand the growth of hundreds of thousands of TikTok fans. Believe it or not, it was a job well done. Regardless, in the realm of TikTok, the difference between a mindless swipe and a tap of the finger to save a video can make or break your business.

For a comprehensive overview of TikTok marketing, see Sprout Social's Complete Guide for Beginners. Account creation includes everything from opening a business account to creating content and even assessing performance.

That is why you can use it as a one-stop shop for learning how TikTok marketing works. Hootsuite also provides a more extensive TikTok Marketing solution, complete with videos, quizzes, and practical exercises to learn from.

In essence, it appears to be more of an online course that explains core platform elements such as content production, communicating with the target audience, and data analysis - all of which are essential for TikTok visibility. Another strategy to spread knowledge among employees is to supply Thanos with updates on impending trends and creative strategies.

Ai blogs are useful to rely on. There are fresh suggestions and examples in this section that provide light on effective TikTok strategy. It's almost as if you're getting the most up-to-date marketing methods for TikTok.

Metricool goes even further, offering a collection of relevant resources based on blogs, e-books, and webinars on how to advertise on TikTok. Take the time to read their resources for an overview of the algorithm, the depth of advertising strategies, and even optimization techniques to become a TikTok expert.

10.3. Benefits of Comprehensive Educational Resources

Spending time on effective and comprehensive teaching materials about TikTok marketing has numerous advantages. First and foremost, such structure guides and courses provide a thorough understanding of the platform's qualities, audience, and advertising opportunities.

This type of information is required to develop material that appeals to the audience and accomplishes the desired results within the TikTok community. That is why instructional resources are more than just theories; they also include advice, specific cases, and examples. They are a transfer of knowledge from theory to real-world experience, tactics that can be used in your TikTok marketing campaigns.

This is because, like most social media sites, the environment is dynamic and ever-changing, with new features and variations being published regularly. Professional information sources become a means of obtaining updated data and determining how to leverage TikTok's procedures for marketing purposes.

Although the usage of such resources is becoming more common in marketing, it results in the enhancement of specialized strategies in a given industry. The following optimization can enhance engagement rates, conversion rates, and thus return on investment (ROI) for your TikTok commercials.

As one is exposed to knowledge and approaches for using TikTok in educational resources, one gains confidence in one's capacity to make reasonable decisions about the app. This confidence enables you to think outside the box, test new thoughts, optimize based on findings and results, and produce consistent results in campaigns. Reading and interacting with marketing materials always leads to social networks of similar marketers.

These communities provide tools, networking opportunities, and a forum for discussing ideas and best practices in TikTok marketing, all of which contribute to the ongoing improvement of the platform.

These ideas also involve mechanical connections to other commerce professionals and marketers in current instructional materials.

Networking also allows for the exchange of ideas, the discovery of new ideas, and the formation of working connections with others in the hostile environment of TikTok marketing. Self-education appeals to official instructional resources boost the ability to work on content development, user interaction, data analysis, and TikTok-specific planning.

These talents are transportable and will help you adjust to the changing needs of digital marketing.

This way, marketers may gain an almost complete understanding of the app, allowing them to approach it confidently and experiment with different content forms, trends, and strategies on TikTok. This is vital today to remain relevant to target groups and contact them through ever-changing social media channels.

TikTok marketing education can be viewed as laying the groundwork for a long-term return on investment. Experience and expertise gained from educational tools prepare you to handle challenges, capitalize on emerging possibilities, and consistently create excellent outcomes for your brand or business on TikTok.

The strong demand for educational resources and marketing tips via TikTok demonstrates the platform's importance in the industry. Marketers can educate themselves and improve their ability to market their businesses on TikTok by being familiar with the available ebooks, online guides, courses, and other learning tools.

Even if you're new to marketing or a seasoned pro, adding these educational materials to your TikTok marketing strategy will increase your chances of success and expand your brand's profile on the site.

Thus, according to TikTok's evolution, it is vital to be updated and educated to compete on such an ever-changing and rapidly evolving platform. TikTok marketers need to understand the TikTok Algorithm, how to create and optimize company accounts, how to create content on the TikTok platform, and how to measure marketing performance.

CHAPTER 11

Avoiding Common Pitfalls

Well done; you have managed to brush up on the basics, create some excellent content, and possibly even go viral. Now that you've relaxed, let me remind you of the TikTok app's hidden risks that may harm you.

Consider this information transfer session to be a conversation with friends in which we both deliver jokes and critique the mistakes that others make. I assure you, do not fall into those traps; they will cost you time and may even turn you red in the face. Are you prepared to avoid certain TikTok landmines? Let's plunge in!

11.1. Common Mistakes and How to Avoid Them

Despite being dubbed the world's playground due to the creative freedom it provides, the terrain is rather slippery. In other words, it is quite easy to become lost in the world of TikTok and appear to be stepping on mine at some point. Because the store has a distinct cultural flavor and operates in a highly competitive environment, mistakes are common. But don't worry; we're here for you!

Here are some of the most common mistakes that individuals make when using the program, as well as things to avoid:

First, ignore trends. TikTok exists under the umbrella of trends, and not following them is like bypassing the main attraction at a social gathering. Participate in trending challenges and employ popular noises to make your account more relevant and visible on the platform.

The biggest mistake you can make on TikTok is not following trends. Still, I'll emphasize that trends are the platform's pulse, and managing them can significantly boost your visibility.

To prevent making this error, pay close attention to the Discover tab or trending hashtags in this mobile app. Interact with the current trends and include trending sounds in your videos. This being a code, you should always remember that timing is everything, and the earlier you get onto a particular trend, the better it will be for you.

Next, with so much stuff competing for viewers' attention, poor video quality is an easy way to turn them off. Shaky footage, poor lighting, and imprecise audio can all take away from your message. To avoid this, consider investing in basic equipment such as a tripod and a ring light.

Even basic modifications, such as cutting superfluous bits and adding captions, can improve the overall quality of your movie. Likewise, overcomplicating content. Simplicity frequently triumphs on TikTok. You do not need a Hollywood production; simply focus on clear, engaging, and honest content. A simple, well-executed notion may resonate more than a complex one.

The initial few seconds of your video are often regarded as the most important. People will skim content that does not immediately capture their attention. The first step in creating a decent video is to capture the audience's interest in your production.

If you've succeeded with the hook, keep in mind that TikTok videos that tell a story perform better than those that don't. For example, a film in which the creative components are solely advertising a product or dancing can be rather uninteresting. To avoid this, include storytelling in your videos.

It could be an anecdote, a backstage, or a story; if something has a story, it catches the audience's attention and makes the content more shareable.

In addition, everything is essential for getting content viewed on TikTok, especially hashtags. However, some people use too many or no hashtags that are relevant to the subject of their creations. As a precaution, never rely exclusively on popular hashtags, but rather use a mix of trending / general hashtags and those unique to the material you're posting. In this regard, it is vital to determine which hashtags are currently popular in the market and modify them for your specific market interest.

This is how TikTok learns and increases the popularity of filmed videos within the appropriate demographic.

This is one of the faults that people might make when using TikTok, and it can significantly hinder their growth. In this situation, followers expect frequent updates, and if they are provided with a random schedule, they will tune out. To prevent this, create a content calendar and adhere to it. Assume TikTok is a TV show that people watch because they know there is something fresh. As a result, it is critical to establish a specific time for posting to keep followers interested.

When posting, it is best to plan your posts so that they are done daily, every two days, or weekly. It thus aids in the development of a strong clientele base by establishing a consistent and ongoing relationship with its customers.

This is something that should be avoided while dealing with analytics. Unquestionably, TikTok provides insights into what is excellent and terrible. Unfortunately, I've seen that many creators do not use
TikTok's statistics services.

Avoiding this requires flying in the dark. To avoid this, it is recommended that you regularly monitor the analytics for information on the audience, videos, and engagement rates. With this in mind, you should gear your content toward the things that interest the viewers most.

Nowadays, it is necessary to use elements borrowed from other successful pages, although copying is not the greatest option. Audiences may immediately identify false content, which, given how TikTok works, will not be favored by the algorithm.

To avoid this, a focus should be placed on the development of personal approaches and strategies. Accept trends, but add a twist. The audience values relatability, which contributes to the platform's unique brand identity.

However, when taken to the extreme, it becomes unproductive, almost like a disability, a negative. In the same way, being overly fixated on perfection might hold you back. As a result, TikTok is not a forum for perfectionism since it is not what it sells.

Do not allow yourself to be held back by the assumption that a particular post is imperfect and hence should not be published. It is often beneficial to make spontaneous postings rather than scheduled posts that receive less involvement from the audience.

Last but not least, people forget to have fun. TikTok is a platform for pleasure and creativity. If you lose interest, it will show in your job, so constantly make sure you appreciate what you are doing. Be yourself, have fun, and so will your audience.

11.2. Navigating TikTok's Community Guidelines

It is also worth noting that it may take some time to read and grasp TikTok's community norms, but it is critical to ensure consistency in uploading when intending to use the app in the long run.

In actuality, TikTok prohibits in-app purchases for accounts that do not meet the age requirement for purchasing the In-app purchase function. This section of the article will discuss the key features of these guidelines and guide on how to prevent potential issues.

The first step that a user should do before exploring the TikTok community guidelines is to familiarize themselves with the basics. For this reason, TikTok maintains the following regulations, which regulate the type of content that can be posted: TikTok is designed to be positive exclusively, so negative stuff is not permitted.

This includes racism, bullying, module fabrics, violence, gore, and sexually explicit content. Furthermore, content that disparages or mocks individuals or groups based on their race, ethnic origin, religion, gender, sexual orientation, or disability is not permitted.

To prevent being targeted by the TikTok police, you should be aware of the following key criteria when creating content: Along with wild jokes and cussing, it is also reasonable to conclude that it is preferable to create content that will not startle people, particularly youngsters.

Today, equipped with social media buttons, incorrect information is transmitted, which might cause harm. TikTok has recently shown activity in the fight against bogus news, which can be seen positively. To avoid being caught up in this, constantly double-check information before passing it on. If you're writing news, numbers, or any other material, be sure it's from a reliable source.

Never feed the accounts with conspiracy theories or general rumors, since this will catch the attention of the moderators and result in your account being blocked. Informing people with accurate information not only helps them trust you but also ensures that the platform remains truthful.

There are various traps to avoid, one of which is a disregard for intellectual property issues. In their policies, they place a high value on intellectual property and have put in place safeguards to ensure that it is not violated. This simply implies that one should not utilize music, films, or other materials that he or she does not own or has not been granted permission to use.

To avoid this, use the music and sound library that TikTok is famous for by obtaining licenses for it. If third-party content can be utilized on your website, make sure you have the permission to use it. This is not only safe under specific conditions, but it also does not violate other people's rights to their work.

TikTok's platforms have a zero-tolerance policy against harassment and bullying. This includes any violation of the privacy of other users, such as harassment, threats, or harsh language. Thus, in order to stay within the confines of emotional expressiveness, courteous conversation must be established while avoiding consequences and negative behavior.

TikTok provides reporting and blocking capabilities that should be used if someone is harassed by another user. It fosters a friendly environment for all because building a positive community relies on supporting the material being shared.

TikTok, like any other social media platform, prioritizes the safety of minors, as evidenced by its main screen. Anything that could damage or sexually abuse minors is frowned upon on social media.

Harassment, sexual ideas or materials directed at toddlers, adolescents, or teenagers, and any type of child cruelty are all prohibited. This is especially vital if your content includes youngsters; make sure it is appropriate for their age and that you have permission. When creating videos with children, remember to follow the do's and don'ts of kid safety and privacy.

Users' privacy is always a concern on social media platforms, including the TikTok app. The standards are also high with concern about the privacy of consumers. Audiences should not contribute any personal information to your videos or include information about others in them. This includes addresses, phone numbers, and other sensitive information. Also, avoid recording other people in public or private settings where they may feel uncomfortable. Protecting people's privacy guarantees that the community being built is trustworthy and reputable.

Finally, acquiring false account followers and likes, as well as generating spam and fake traffic, are all prohibited. This includes fabricating likes, views and followers using false bots or accounts. There is nothing wrong with desiring a more organic feel to your account while using the site, but attempting to bypass this regulation will result in your account being banned.

Concentrating on providing outstanding material that organically promotes interaction with the website or feed is sufficient. Engagement with your audience is considerably more beneficial than false stuff, and it will prove more effective in the long term. One can agree that it is critical to understand and follow the rules governing the TikTok community.

As a result, you can not only save your profile but also engage in constructive conversations on Tumblr and work to enhance the website's overall tone. Remember these principles while you develop and share your material; keep in mind that while TikTok's presence is strong, it must be used responsibly.

11.3. Dealing with Negative Feedback

TikTok, like any other social media platform, is going to attract unfavorable feedback. You must understand how to use it correctly for your health and to maintain a positive online presence. In this essay, I'll describe how to respond to bad comments on TikTok.

To begin, one must discern between constructive criticism and destructive criticism. When others say things to you that you don't like or are harsh, the roughness usually serves to help you improve your work.

Focus on comments that provide specific recommendations on what needs to be done. These are the channels of expansion. Similarly, trolling or hate speech often has nobody and should be disregarded with contempt. Consider it an opportunity to upgrade and improve your technique based on client preferences.

When dealing with distractions, be courteous and formal. It is important to respond to the comment constructively, acknowledging that the commenter's opinion is valid, even if it varies from yours.

Do not dispute because it is unhelpful and may exacerbate the problem. However, do not oppose him or her by claiming that your opinion is correct, but rather demonstrate your appreciation for his or her opinion and willingness to listen and compromise.

If one wishes to transition from negative to good communication, one must find the correct words and be attentive. This demonstrates assessments and drive to change, which might benefit you in terms of your audience's attitudes.

In particular, it is vital to avoid replying to every unfavorable evaluation. As a result, one can publish irrelevant comments, based on assumptions, or even intended to stir up controversy. In such cases, it is preferable to ignore such individuals than to pay them any attention. There is a need to follow constructive advice, which includes replies that are valuable and should be investigated.

As previously stated, your time is effectively spent here in developing and keeping a strong relationship with your audience.

If a comment is abusive, obscene, harassing, or expresses hatred, it should be reported. TikTok has safeguards in place to address inappropriate behavior. Such remarks should be recorded to prevent the community from becoming antagonistic to all members.

Furthermore, because those who overwhelm their page with negativity will not be welcome back, other legitimate users will not be harassed, and the page will become a nicer place.

Another effective method is to use negative feedback as material for content creation. Respond to the channel's general complaints with a new video, and turn a performance failure into a learning opportunity. It also serves to reassure your audience that you have heard them, but it also demonstrates your ability to deal with constructive criticism.

Similarly, when dealing with negativity, one must also be mindful of their well-being. Staying up to speed on news has ramifications, as negativity can be harmful to one's physical and mental health. If you are bothered by the comments, try not to read them, and avoid those who will say such things to you. Remember that anonymous individuals on computers and other screens do not create value.

Finally, try to focus on your strengths. While you may get a few unfavorable comments about your product, I am sure there are many positive ones. Self-congratulate and be grateful for the humane people of the community. Thus, focusing on positive feedback for your videos or comments can be beneficial because it makes you and those who follow you happy.

In short, dealing with negative feedback entails keeping a positive attitude and continuing to enhance the director's ability. Accepting these problems as normal occurrences in the development process will enable the business to improve its performance. Recognize accomplishments, big or small; every step is important and should be documented. So, by maintaining a good attitude and a desire to improve your talents, you will be able to effectively navigate TikTok's hurdles.

11.4. Staying Updated with Platform Changes
Staying up to date on TikTok platform upgrades is critical for maintaining the success of the program. TikTok frequently adds new features, adjusts algorithms, and changes its policies, so staying up to date with the latest updates will allow you to get the most out of TikTok.

To begin, TikTok has an official blog and news update area, which I believe is quite useful to read regularly. It's also worth noting that TikTok periodically makes large announcements about upcoming major updates, new features, or policy changes on its official sites.

Such upgrades may include new features, modifications to existing algorithms, or changes to community policies. In this manner, you will receive a direct feed from the tonne, allowing you to be notified promptly when updates occur.

Another option is to join TikTok creator communities and obtain advice from them. These communities can be found on social media platforms such as Twitter, Facebook, and Reddit, and they are populated by creators who share advice, updates, and innovations.

As a result, joining these organizations will sharpen your skills because other designers may have previously used the trend or feature. TikTok artists and notable celebrities discuss platform developments in their material.

If you can identify a few popular TikTokers, watch how they handle the situation and apply the update or new feature. These producers use the products of these sectors first and provide you with a template to draw from.

It is also a good idea to try out new features as they become available. For example, you may observe people testing Facebook's new features. TikTok regularly refreshes its editing tools, filters, and effects.

Using these options early in the content development process allows you to easily search for different methods to attach features to your movies. Furthermore, because TikTok is always upgrading its options, two, employing new options will increase your account's popularity; three, TikTok's algorithm despises inactive users; and four, TikTok's algorithm despises false followers.

It will also be beneficial to regularly learn about algorithm updates. The following shows how TikTok's recommendation system determines what you see. Do not disregard emerging trends and adapt your strategy accordingly. Updating your material regularly will keep it relevant and, as a result, more noticeable.

Reading about the current industry trends and following social media marketing will help you obtain a broader view of TikTok and other apps.

Some of these sources examine patterns and changes across multiple social media platforms, providing a more comprehensive view of social media content. The ideas let you predict change and respond to it promptly within your content production strategy.

Interacting with the network's help and feedback areas can also be useful. If you do not understand some of the new functions or modifications, you can clarify them by contacting TikTok support or reading the help center section. Furthermore, offering input is effective in shaping future upgrades to the platform for the benefit of the producers.

Changing the platform is a constant process. Make a timetable for yourself so that you can keep up with TikTok changes and participate in the community. These preventive actions will help you remain ahead and be better prepared to adapt to any changes that the platform may bring, both now and in the future.

To keep up with TikTok's platform changes, you must engage in the following activities: public announcements, following creators, participating in communities, tracking industries and influencers, using new features, algorithm knowledge, and external sources.

This allows one to remain relevant and successful on TikTok while also utilizing new promising tools that appear to increase content and attract more people.

CHAPTER 12

Future Trends and Opportunities.
Amid the rapid currents of social media apps, TikTok doesn't follow trends—it creates them. This chapter explores Tiktok's future, including features such as sophisticated shopping and bespoke content, as well as the transition to virtual reality.

Considering these concepts, TikTok not only alters existing trends but also offers new avenues for creators and marketers to connect with their audiences.

Whether you're a creative genius or a marketing machine, keeping an eye out for these new developments can help you stand out in the fast-paced TikTok environment. With changing times and trends, as well as technological advancements, this social media platform remains relevant and full of opportunities for self-expression.

Make way for TikTok, the next era's social media craze, with all of its new features and every single second on the app ready for new users to shape the new digital reality.

12.1 Emerging Trends on TikTok
Okay, get down to business. TikTok is rapidly expanding, and some truly incredible trends are poised to shape its future. And if you want to have a powerful, unparalleled influence in your market, you should look into these. Regarding AR filters, let me state the following.

They're exploding up! TikTok AR filters allow you to modify the background of your videos and add a variety of interesting and interactive components. And, guess what? They are only growing better and more entertaining, so your content can be spectacular.

However, TikTok users can do more than just mock the viral dance challenges; it is also becoming a learning platform.

Audiences are abandoning it in favor of minute-long films, content that claims to teach a new skill quickly, and the like. Are you hungry and want to prepare a new meal, learn a new language, or see some amazing science experiments?

TikTok has you covered when it comes to both entertaining and educational stuff. Collaborative compositions and duets are also presented differently. The duet function allows you to create side-by-side videos with another individual, making it easy to cooperate and/or build a following. Artist collaborations will grow cooler and more unpredictable as creators seek out more creative duos.

Sustainability is also becoming increasingly popular. The majority of people care about the environment, and TikTok is no different.

Every artist wants to share important information about environmental conservation or the use of eco-friendly products. What appears to be a trend is a truly wonderful shift. To add, interactive challenges? It is still a significant irritation, although they are becoming more engaged.

These challenges, whether they be lighthearted bouts or stunning dance wars, are ideal for expressing oneself and engaging the audience. Furthermore, it is advantageous because businesses have now dived into the fun-note, making obstacles a clear plus.

Live streaming is another rapidly growing trend. Because TikTok Live is an efficient tool for communication with the audience, numerous activities that can be held in real-time are as interesting as possible: Q&As, performances, and many more. To be honest, it's an impressive method to build a loyal following. Furthermore, one cannot overlook integration with e-commerce possibilities.

Recently, there have been a lot of enhancements to features that allow users to buy without leaving the TikTok site, yes, without leaving the site. The makers can tag a product, and anyone who watches the film can quickly purchase it. The concept is to be able to pretend to shop, but much more thrilling and fancy.

Special interest groups are also doing well. Regardless of whether it is books for nerds, workout routines or some niche interest, there is a tribe for that on TikTok. These communities are really useful for finding your target audience and developing content that will align with them. Another interesting aspect is related to health.

Mental health and self-care content are also increasing dramatically. As more people in society talk about mental health, more TikTok content makers are willing to share their stories, tips, and encouragement with others. It allows for a positive environment in which one can be encouraged and find someone to advise him or her. It should be known that this cuts across other general issues.

Lastly, it is beneficial to point out that the general idea of AI and personalization is only advancing at its pace. It reveals that TikTok is getting even smarter in understanding your preference so you can watch as many videos as you want, and you will never get bored.

To sum it up, TikTok is quite chaotic with trends coming and going. Keep up with what's hot and make sure you incorporate them into your content plan to rule the platform.

12.2. Preparing for the Future of TikTok
So, if you want to stand out and be one of the most popular content makers, then read on. When it comes to planning operations, strategy is vital, yet you must also be flexible. The platform is constantly shifting, and the only way we can stay relevant and in control is to identify those shifts and learn how to capitalize on those chances.

To begin, always stick to navigation and the most recent TikTok trends. Maintain a regular visit to TikTok's Blog and stay up to date on industry news and content creators. Knowing what is new allows the user to take advantage of the new tools and topics, it is fun to have fresh content.

Now, let's discuss skills and creativity", I said to the guys. The latest developments that TikTok is implementing include AR, VR, as well as AI, and these you must follow.

Take time and try to research these technologies and try to find ways on how they can be incorporated into your videos. The more proficient you become in these, the higher the distinction of your content will be.

Another significant aspect is the promotion of a personal brand. Given TikTok's change to a confirmed particular target population and a focus on individual personalized content, having a cohesive and concise brand image is even more vital. Be clear about how you want your page to look, how you want to write, and what your ideals are, and make sure to reflect them in all of your postings.

Solid is the type of brand that allows you to be quickly recognized and remembered, which is desirable. Do not focus on a specific type of information. Diversify!

Sure, explore deeper, but don't be scared to experiment. Sprinkle it with instructive content, vlogs that show how things are made, or collaborations with other content creators.

It is something you should seriously consider while monetizing your TikTok account.

Examine the brand collaborations, native ads, and buy-now buttons. TikTok is moving more towards e-commerce, and being prepared to capitalize on any of these opportunities will boost your revenue stream. Stay educated to ensure you have the most up-to-date information on the platform's many ways of making money and how to incorporate them into your strategy.

Finally, keep track of your analytics because these are vital aspects to consider. TikTok provides several capabilities that might help you analyze your audience and the performance of your posts; these are known as analytics. Check your analytics once a week to evaluate what is and is not effective. Use this information to alter your content strategy, make changes to videos to increase your audience, and make good decisions about future releases.

Thus, to prepare for TikTok's future, it is critical to be informed, improve, brand, communicate, vary, earn, and count. With these procedures to become prepared and follow the preceding advice, you'll be armed to deal with TikTok's ever-changing environment and continue to thrive on this consistently shifting platform.

12.3. Expanding Your Brand Beyond TikTok
Very good, let me tell you more about TikTok's current status outside of its dancing platform. Yes, TikTok is wonderful for expanding your brand, but if you want to take it a step further and gain as much awareness as possible, you must diversify.

You should consider expanding your social networks. Open a shop on Instagram, YouTube, and Twitch; they are all distinct, and various individuals use them.

Target it to each first, based on their specialties and what is popular among their respective audiences. This way, you're not simply sticking with a narrow group of people; you're broadening your horizons in each area.

For example, suppose you run a fashion brand that is popular on TikTok due to its fashionable streetwear. To increase your reach, you decide to diversify across platforms. Instagram allows you to share high-resolution images and collaborate with fashion influencers.

YouTube becomes your go-to source for behind-the-scenes films, styling advice, and vlogs aimed at fashion aficionados seeking in-depth information. By proactively broadening your presence across these platforms, you not only increase your brand's visibility but also appeal to a wide range of customer tastes and behaviors, resulting in more brand awareness and engagement across demographics.

A precise alignment of all promised values is required to maintain a consistent brand image. This way, prospects will see that you own all of [the aforementioned platforms] and that your voice, appearance, and messaging are consistent. Consistency pays off and makes you known, so whether customers come across your content on Facebook, YouTube, Twitter, or any other site, they quickly recognize you and your principles.

When you manage to promote your work over as many platforms as possible. Replicate the content perfectly on your TikTok accounts, and reciprocate on Instagram, YouTube, and other social media channels. Emphasize what is available on one platform but not on the other, such as unreleased content, a backstage pass, or an interaction.

This encourages your followers to check you out on platforms other than the one they communicate with you on, thereby expanding your audience.

Do not neglect your digital footprints. Creating a website or blog is not terrible at all because it serves as the foundation for everything that is built around a brand. It's where customers can learn more about you, explore more sections, and perhaps buy your products or services.

Furthermore, the process of optimizing your website for search engines will most likely generate organic web visits in addition to social media traffic.

And, let's not overlook the offline world. What about SMEs and other businesses that do not use the internet for business? Most industry insiders, emerging stars, and others will see you in your element when you participate in events such as industry events, trade exhibits, fairs, and local community events relating to your wing.

The advantages of networking in this manner include making personal contact, knowing the environment in the sphere, and displaying the brand's tone of voice outside of the keyboard.

So, to expand your brand outside of TikTok, you should be on other social networks, maintain aesthetic consistency, distribute content on other platforms, repost content, collaborate with influencers, create a website/blog, and network in person. This allows you to reach a larger audience and make your brand more recognizable, which will help its long-term success.

12.4 Anticipating Future Trends
In this case, predicting the future of social media generally or planning for the future of TikTok is like aiming at a dart board in the dark but based on the existing trends, some good guesstimates can be made. While they weren't necessarily bad, one big

area to watch was the speed at which they were rolling out ideas. Online shopping.

Thus, TikTok may introduce even more entertaining e-commerce features soon. Picture this: includes online shopping through augmented reality and this can include taking clothes trials or seeing where a piece of furniture will fit in your house before ordering for it. : Included in constant suggestions following your interests and even your browsing history, it brings the whole concept of how brands engage with us and even make direct sales within the application to the next level.

In this instance, predicting the future of social media in general or planning for the future of TikTok is similar to aiming at a dart board in the dark, although some solid estimates can be made based on current patterns. While they weren't inherently horrible, one thing to keep an eye on was how quickly they were implementing suggestions. Online shopping.

TikTok may soon add even more amusing e-commerce services. Picture this: involves online shopping through augmented reality (AR), which might entail doing clothes trials or visualizing where a piece of furniture will go in your house before acquiring it.: Included in frequent suggestions based on your hobbies and even your browsing history, it brings the whole concept of how brands engage with us and even make direct sales within the application to the next level.

Other areas of investment finance are Note: exciting include. If pressed further, advancements in artificial intelligence (AI) represent another interesting subject for investment funding. As a result, with the use of AI, TikTok's ability to adapt to each user may improve even further.

Thus, using your data and activities, the program may show you material that appears to be tailored specifically to you, making you feel happier and more engaged. For advertisers, this implies more targeting, and users, well, they're more happy, don't you think?

However, these trends are still in the possibilities phase at the moment. All of their realizations shall therefore be dictated by the developments of technology, the wishes of users, and the specific developments of this application known as TikTok.

Yet by keeping abreast of the existing and constantly evolving trends, the brands can strategically align themselves to benefit from such opportunities as informed by social media's dynamic nature.

Moreover, these tendencies are still at the potential stage at the present. All of their realizations will be influenced by technological advancements, user preferences, and the specific advances of the TikTok application. However, by staying current with present and ever-changing trends, brands can strategically align themselves to capitalize on such opportunities as informed by the dynamic nature of social media platforms.

What's the takeaway here? To flourish on TikTok and other developing platforms, businesses must be adaptable and future-proofed. Because of these characteristics, marketers must constantly monitor the platform for changes. Stay up to date on current trends and new features, try out fresh ideas, and use all of TikTok's available capabilities to achieve long-term success.

As a result, it will assist you in maintaining attention to your brand in TikTok's ever-changing environment and predicting key adjustments that may be seamlessly integrated into your plan.

When used consistently, the aforementioned tactics can help you establish a sustainable and original marketing viewpoint that will function effectively for skilled, sophisticated, and multicultural audiences. Therefore, keep wondering, keep evolving, and be open to embracing the next thing TikTok has in store for you!

www.ingramcontent.com/pod-product-compliance
Lightning Source LLC
Chambersburg PA
CBHW052154220526
45471CB00004B/1678